NELSON DENNY FOR POLICE

COMPLETE STUDY GUIDE AND PRACTICE TEST QUESTIONS

Copyright Notice

Copyright © 2021 by Complete Test Preparation Inc. ALL RIGHTS RESERVED. No part of this book may be reproduced or transferred in any form or by any means, graphic, electronic, or mechanical, including photocopying, recording, web distribution, taping, or by any information storage retrieval system, without the written permission of the author.

Notice: Complete Test Preparation makes every reasonable effort to obtain from reliable sources accurate, complete, and timely information about the tests covered in this book. Nevertheless, changes can be made in the tests or the administration of the tests at any time and Complete Test Preparation makes no representation or warranty, either expressed or implied as to the accuracy, timeliness, or completeness of the information contained in this book. Complete Test Preparation make no representations or warranties of any kind, express or implied, about the completeness, accuracy, reliability, suitability or availability with respect to the information contained in this document for any purpose. Any reliance you place on such information is therefore strictly at your own risk.

The author(s) shall not be liable for any loss incurred as a consequence of the use and application, directly or indirectly, of any information presented in this work. Sold with the understanding, the author is not engaged in rendering professional services or advice. If advice or expert assistance is required, the services of a competent professional should be sought.

The company, product and service names used in this publication are for identification purposes only. All trademarks and registered trademarks are the property of their respective owners. Complete Test Preparation is not affiliated with any educational institution.

We strongly recommend that students check with exam providers for up-to-date information regarding test content.

ISBN-13: 9781772454703

Version 9 March 2025

Published by
Complete Test Preparation Inc.
Victoria BC Canada
Visit us on the web at https://www.test-preparation.ca
Printed in the USA

About Complete Test Preparation Inc.

Why Us?
The Complete Test Preparation Team has been publishing high quality study materials since 2005, with a catalogue of over 145 titles, in English, French and Chinese, as well as ESL curriculum for all levels.

To keep up with the industry changes, we update everything all the time!

And the best part?
With every purchase, you're helping people all over the world improve themselves and their education. So thank you in advance for supporting this mission with us! Together, we are truly making a difference in the lives of those often forgotten by the system.

Charities that we support -
https://www.test-preparation.ca/charities-and-non-profits/

You have definitely come to the right place.
If you want to spend your valuable study time where it will help you the most - we've got you covered today and tomorrow.

https://www.facebook.com/CompleteTestPreparation/

https://www.youtube.com/user/MrTestPreparation

Contents

6	**Getting Started with the Nelson Denny**	
9	**Reading Comprehension**	
	Self Assessment	12
	Answer Key	18
	Help with Reading Comprehension	21
	Drawing Inferences And Conclusions	26
29	**Vocabulary**	
	Self Assessment	32
	Answer Key	35
36	**Nelson Denny Practice Test Questions**	
	Answer Key	61
71	**Practice Test Questions Set 2**	
	Answer Key	93
103	**Practice Tests 3 & 4**	
104	**How to Improve your Vocabulary**	
	Meaning in Context	107
	The Top 100 Common Vocabulary	112
	Stem Words	114
	Stem Words Practice Questions	120
	Stem Words Practice Part II	132
	Most Common Prefix	137
	Prefix Questions	140
	Most Common Synonyms	145
	Synonym Practice Questions	150
	Most Common Antonyms	155
	Antonym Practice Questions	160
165	**How to Prepare for a Test**	
169	**How to Take a Test**	
	Reading the Instructions	169
	How to Take a Test - The Basics	170
	In the Test Room – What you MUST do!	172
	Avoid Anxiety Before a Test	175
	Common Test-Taking Mistakes	176
178	**Conclusion**	
179	**Online Resources**	

Getting Started with the Nelson Denny

CONGRATULATIONS! By deciding to take the Nelson Denny Reading Test, (NDRT) you have taken the first step toward a great future! Of course, there is no point in taking this important examination unless you intend to do your best to earn the highest grade you possibly can. That means getting yourself organized and discovering the best approaches, methods and strategies to master the material. Yes, that will require real effort and dedication, but if you are willing to focus your energy and devote the study time necessary, before you know it you will be opening that letter of acceptance to the school of your dreams.

We know that taking on a new endeavour can be scary, and it is easy to feel unsure of where to begin. That's where we come in. This study guide is designed to help you improve your test-taking skills, show you a few tricks and increase both your competency and confidence.

The Nelson Denny Exam

The Nelson Denny has two subject areas, reading comprehension and vocabulary. Since how well you score in each of these areas will determine if you get into the best school possible, it is important to be prepared. In the area of reading comprehension, examinees will be tested on their ability to comprehend reading passages, make inferences regarding those passages and draw logical conclusions. In the vocabulary section you will be tested on your word knowledge.

How this Study Guide is Organized

This study guide is divided into four sections. The first section, Getting Started, gives basic information about the Nelson Denny and how to make a study plan and schedule.

The second section, Self-Assessments will help you recognize your areas of strength and weakness. This will be a boon when it comes to managing your study time most efficiently; there is not much point of focusing on material you already have firmly under control. Instead, taking the self-assessments will show you where that time could be much better spent. The Self-Assessments have a few questions to evaluate quickly your understanding of material similar to what you will find on the Nelson Denny. If you do poorly in certain areas, simply work carefully through those sections in the tutorials and then try the self-assessment again.

The third section contains two sets of practice test questions with questions similar in type and difficulty to the Nelson Denny.

The fourth is an in-depth Tutorial on how to improve your vocabulary. If you are reading this book and studying for the Nelson Denny, you probably don't have time to use the most effective way to increase your vocabulary, which is reading all the time. Therefore, things being what they are, we offer fast and effective strategies for increasing your vocabulary, as well as two hundred practice questions.

While we seek to make our guide as comprehensive as possible, note that like all exams, the Nelson Denny Exam might be adjusted at some future point. New material might be added, or content that is no longer relevant or applicable might be removed. It is always a good idea to give the materials you receive when you register to take the Nelson Denny a careful review.

The Nelson Denny Exam Study Plan

Now that you have made the decision to take the Nelson Denny, it is time to get started. Before you do another thing, you will need to figure out a plan of attack. The very best study tip is to start early! The longer you devote to regular study practice, the more likely you will retain the material and access it quickly, and under stressful situations - like in an exam room! If you thought that 1 X 20 is the same as 2 X 10, guess what? It really is not, when it comes to study time. Reviewing material for just an hour per day over the course of 20 days is far better than studying for two hours a day for only 10 days. The more often you revisit a particular piece of information, the better you will know it. Not only will your grasp and understanding be better, but your ability to reach into your brain and quickly and efficiently pull out the tidbit you need, will be greatly enhanced as well.

The great Chinese scholar and philosopher Confucius believed that true knowledge could be defined as knowing what you know and what you do not know. The first step in preparing for the Nelson Denny Exam is to assess your strengths and weaknesses. You may already have an idea of what you know and what you do not know, but evaluating yourself using our Self- Assessment modules for both Vocabulary and Reading Comprehension, will clarify the details.

MAKING A STUDY SCHEDULE

To make your study time the most productive, you will need to develop a study plan. The purpose of the plan is to organize all the bits of pieces of information in such a way that you will not feel overwhelmed. Rome was not built in a day, and learning everything you will need to know to pass the Nelson Denny is going to take time, too. Arranging the material you need to learn into manageable chunks is the best way to go. Each study session should take you one step closer to your final goal and make you feel as though you have succeeded in accomplishing something. Your goal is simply to learn what you planned to learn during that particular session. Try to organize the content in such a way that each study session builds on previous ones. That way, you will retain the information, be better able to access it, and review the previous bits and pieces at the same time.

It makes sense to focus your study time on those subjects that need the most work and unless you create a visual chart for yourself, chances are good you will quickly get confused. First, write out what you need to study and how much time you want to devote to it. This is easy since the Nelson Denny is a pretty simple format, with only reading comprehension and vocabulary questions. Next, consider how many days before the test. Plan to take time off from studying on the day before the exam is scheduled. On the last day before the test, you will not learn anything and will probably only confuse yourself. Besides, giving yourself a little break means you will feel fresher on the day of the test.

Make a table with columns for the number of days before the test and rows for the number of hours you have available to study each day. We suggest working with half hour and one hour time slots; less than that means you will get set up to study and it will be time to quit, and more than an hour might result in mental fatigue.

Now you are ready to begin filling in the blanks. Give the most time to those subjects you need to study the most. It is also a good idea to assign your weakest subjects the most regular time slots. In fact, even just thirty minutes a day will help lock in the information you need. Of course, those subjects that you know like the back of your hand can be assigned the shortest blocks of time.

Tips for Making a Study Schedule

Once you set a schedule that works, stick with it! Establish study sessions that are realistic. Blocking out study time that is too long or too short means you will be tempted to cheat. Instead, schedule study sessions that are reasonable and you will set yourself up for success!

Schedule breaks. Breaks are just as important as study time. Work out a rotation of studying and brief breaks that works for you.

Build up study time. If you find it hard to sit still and study for an hour at first, build up to it. Start with 20 minutes, and then take a break. Once you get used to 20-minute study sessions, increase the time to 30 minutes. Gradually work your way up to a full hour.

Forty minutes to an hour is optimal. Studying for longer is not productive. Studying for periods that are too short won't give you enough time to really learn anything.

Reading Comprehension

THIS SECTION CONTAINS A SELF-ASSESSMENT AND READING TUTORIAL. The tutorial is designed to familiarize general principles and the self-assessment contains general questions similar to the reading questions likely to be on the Nelson Denny exam, but are not intended to be identical to the exam questions. The tutorials are not designed to be a complete reading course, and it is assumed that students have some familiarity with reading comprehension questions. If you do not understand parts of the tutorial, or find the tutorial difficult, it is recommended that you seek out additional instruction.

Note that these questions are for skill practice only.

Tour of the Nelson Denny Reading Content

Below is a more detailed list of the types of reading questions that generally appear on the Nelson Denny.

- Drawing logical conclusions
- Identify the author's intent, e.g. to persuade, inform, entertain, etc.
- Make predictions
- Give the definition of a word from context

The questions below are not the same as you will find on the Nelson Denny - that would be too easy! And nobody knows what the questions will be and they change all the time. Mostly the changes consist of substituting new questions for old, but the changes can be new question formats or styles, changes to the number of questions in each section, changes to the time limits for each section and combining sections. Below are general reading questions that cover the same areas as the Nelson Denny. So, while the format and exact wording of the questions may differ slightly, and change from year to year, if you can answer the questions below, you will have no problem with the reading section of the Nelson Denny.

Reading Self-Assessment

The purpose of the self-assessment is:

- Identify your strengths and weaknesses.
- Develop your personalized study plan (above)
- Get accustomed to the Nelson Denny format
- Extra practice – the self-assessments are almost a full 3rd practice test!

- Provide a baseline score for preparing your study schedule.

Since this is a self-assessment, and depending on how confident you are with reading comprehension, timing is optional. The self-assessment has 16 questions, so allow about 20 minutes to complete this assessment.

Once complete, use the table below to assess your understanding of the content, and prepare your study schedule described in chapter 1.

80% - 100%	Excellent – you have mastered the content!
60 – 79%	Good. You have a working knowledge. Even though you can just pass this section, you may want to review the Tutorials and do some extra practice to see if you can improve your mark.
40% - 59%	Below Average. You do not understand reading comprehension problems. Review the tutorials, and retake this quiz again in a few days, before proceeding to the rest of the study guide.
Less than 40%	Poor. You have a very limited understanding of reading comprehension problems. Please review the Tutorials, and retake this quiz again in a few days, before proceeding to the rest of the study guide.

ANSWER SHEET

1. Ⓐ Ⓑ Ⓒ Ⓓ   11. Ⓐ Ⓑ Ⓒ Ⓓ
2. Ⓐ Ⓑ Ⓒ Ⓓ   12. Ⓐ Ⓑ Ⓒ Ⓓ
3. Ⓐ Ⓑ Ⓒ Ⓓ   13. Ⓐ Ⓑ Ⓒ Ⓓ
4. Ⓐ Ⓑ Ⓒ Ⓓ   14. Ⓐ Ⓑ Ⓒ Ⓓ
5. Ⓐ Ⓑ Ⓒ Ⓓ   15. Ⓐ Ⓑ Ⓒ Ⓓ
6. Ⓐ Ⓑ Ⓒ Ⓓ   16. Ⓐ Ⓑ Ⓒ Ⓓ
7. Ⓐ Ⓑ Ⓒ Ⓓ
8. Ⓐ Ⓑ Ⓒ Ⓓ
9. Ⓐ Ⓑ Ⓒ Ⓓ
10. Ⓐ Ⓑ Ⓒ Ⓓ

Directions: The following questions are based on several reading passages. A series of questions follow each passage. Read each passage carefully, and then answer the questions based on it. You may reread the passage as often as you wish. When you have finished answering the questions based on one passage, go right onto the next passage. Choose the best answer based on the information given and implied.

Questions 1 – 4 refer to the following passage.

Passage 1 - Who Was Anne Frank?

You may have heard mention of the word Holocaust in your History or English classes. The Holocaust took place from 1939-1945. It was an attempt by the Nazi party to purify the human race, by eliminating Jews, Gypsies, Catholics, homosexuals and others they deemed inferior to their "perfect" Aryan race. The Nazis used Concentration Camps, which were sometimes used as Death Camps, to exterminate the people they held in the camps. The saddest fact about the Holocaust was the over one million children under the age of sixteen died in a Nazi concentration camp. Just a few weeks before World War II was over, Anne Frank was one of those children to die.

Before the Nazi party began its persecution of the Jews, Anne Frank had a happy life. She was born in June of 1929. In June of 1942, for her 13th birthday, she was given a simple present which would go onto impact the lives of millions of people around the world. That gift was a small red diary that she called Kitty. This diary was to become Anne's most treasured possession when she and her family hid from the Nazis in a secret annex above her father's office building in Amsterdam.

For 25 months, Anne, her sister Margot, her parents, another family, and an elderly Jewish dentist hid from the Nazis in this tiny annex. They were never permitted to go outside, and their food and supplies were brought to them by Miep Gies and her husband, who did not believe in the Nazi persecution of the Jews. It was a very difficult life for young Anne and she used Kitty as an outlet to describe her life in hiding.
After 2 years, Anne and her family were betrayed and arrested by the Nazis. To this day, nobody is exactly sure who betrayed the Frank family and the other annex residents. Anne, her mother, and her sister were separated from Otto Frank, Anne's father. Then, Anne and Margot were separated from their mother. In March of 1945, Margot Frank died of starvation in a Concentration Camp. A few days later, at the age of 15, Anne Frank died of typhus. Of all the people who hid in the Annex, only Otto Frank survived the Holocaust.

Otto Frank returned to the Annex after World War II. It was there that he found Kitty, filled with Anne's thoughts and feelings about being a persecuted Jewish girl. Otto Frank had Anne's diary published in 1947 and it has remained continuously in print ever since. Today, the diary has been published in over 55 languages and more than 24 million copies have been sold around the world. The Diary of Anne Frank tells the story of a brave young woman who tried to see the good in all people.

1. From the context clues in the passage, the word Annex means?

    a. Attic

    b. Bedroom

    c. Basement

    d. Kitchen

2. Why do you think Anne's diary has been published in 55 languages?

    a. So everyone could understand it.

    b. So people around the world could learn more about the horrors of the Holocaust.

    c. Because Anne was Jewish but hid in Amsterdam and died in Germany.

    d. Because Otto Frank spoke many languages.

3. From the description of Anne and Margot's deaths in the passage, what can we assume typhus is?

    a. The same as starving to death.

    b. An infection the Germans gave to Anne.

    c. A disease Anne caught in the concentration camp.

    d. Poison gas used by the Germans to kill Anne.

4. In the third paragraph, what does the word outlet mean?

    a. A place to plug things into the wall

    b. A store where Miep bought cheap supplies for the Frank family

    c. A hiding space similar to an Annex

    d. A place where Anne could express her private thoughts.

Questions 5 – 8 refer to the following passage.

Passage 2 - Was Dr. Seuss A Real Doctor?

A favorite author for over 100 years, Theodor Seuss Geisel was born on March 2, 1902. Today, we celebrate the birthday of the famous "Dr. Seuss" by hosting Read Across America events throughout the March. School children around the country celebrate the "Doctor's" birthday by making hats, giving presentations and holding read aloud circles featuring some of Dr. Seuss' most famous books.

But who was Dr. Seuss? Did he go to medical school? Where was his office? You may be surprised to know that Theodor Seuss Geisel was not a medical doctor at all. He took on the nickname Dr. Seuss when he became a noted children's book author. He earned the nickname because people said his books were "as good as medicine." All these years later, his nickname has lasted and he is known as Dr. Seuss all across the world.

Think back to when you were a young child. Did you ever want to try "green eggs and ham?" Did you try to "Hop on Pop?" Do you remember learning about the environment from a creature called The Lorax? Of course, you must recall one of Seuss' most famous characters; that green Grinch who stole Christmas. These stories were all written by Dr. Seuss and featured his signature rhyming words and letters. They also featured made up words to enhance his rhyme scheme and even though many of his characters were made up, they sure seem real to us today.

And what of his "signature" book, The Cat in the Hat? You must remember that cat and Thing One and Thing Two from your childhood. Did you know that in the early 1950's there was a growing concern in America that children were not becoming avid readers? This was, book publishers thought, because children found books dull and uninteresting. An intelligent publisher sent Dr. Seuss a book of words that he thought all children should learn as young readers. Dr. Seuss wrote his famous story The Cat in the Hat, using those words. We can see, over the decades, just how much influence his writing has had on very young children. That is why we celebrate this doctor's birthday each March.

5. What does the word "avid" mean in the last paragraph?

    a. Good

    b. Interested

    c. Slow

    d. Fast

6. What can we infer from the statement " His books were like medicine?"

    a. His books made people feel better

    b. His books were in doctor's office waiting rooms

    c. His books took away fevers

    d. His books left a funny taste in readers' mouths.

7. Why is the publisher in the last paragraph called "intelligent?"

    a. The publisher knew how to read.

    b. The publisher knew kids did not like to read.

    c. The publisher knew Dr. Seuss would be able to create a book that sold well.

    d. The publisher knew that Dr. Seuss would be able to write a book that would get young children interested in reading.

8. The theme of this passage is

   a. Dr. Seuss was not a doctor.

   b. Dr. Seuss influenced the lives of generations of young children.

   c. Dr. Seuss wrote rhyming books.

   d. Dr. Seuss' birthday is a good day to read a book.

Questions 9 - 11 refer to the following passage.

Keeping Tropical Fish

Keeping tropical fish at home or in your office used to be very popular. Today, interest has declined, but it remains as rewarding and relaxing a hobby as ever. Ask any tropical fish hobbyist, and you will hear how soothing and relaxing watching colorful fish live their lives in the aquarium. If you are considering keeping tropical fish as pets, here is a list of basic equipment you will need.

A filter is essential for keeping your aquarium clean and your fish alive and healthy. There are different types and sizes of filters and the right size for you depends on the size of the aquarium and the level of stocking. Generally, you need a filter with a 3 to 5 times turn over rate per hour. This means that the water in the tank should go through the filter about 3 to 5 times per hour.

Most tropical fish do well in water temperatures ranging between 24^0 C and 26^0 C, though each has its own ideal water temperature. A heater with a thermostat is necessary to regulate the water temperature. Some heaters are submersible and others are not, so check carefully before you buy.

Lights are also necessary, and come in a large variety of types, strengths and sizes. A light source is necessary for plants in the tank to photosynthesize and give the tank a more attractive appearance. Even if you plan to use plastic plants, the fish still require light, although here you can use a lower strength light source.

A hood is necessary to keep dust, dirt and unwanted materials out of the tank. Sometimes the hood can also help prevent evaporation. Another requirement is aquarium gravel. This will improve the aesthetics of the aquarium and is necessary if you plan to have real plants.

9. What is the general tone of this article?

   a. Formal

   b. Informal

   c. Technical

   d. Opinion

10. Which of the following cannot be inferred?

    a. Gravel is good for aquarium plants.

    b. Fewer people have aquariums in their office than at home.

    c. The larger the tank, the larger the filter required.

    d. None of the above.

11. What evidence does the author provide to support their claim that aquarium lights are necessary?

    a. Plants require light.

    b. Fish and plants require light.

    c. The author does not provide evidence for this statement.

    d. Aquarium lights make the aquarium more attractive.

12. Which of the following is an opinion?

    a. Filter with a 3 to 5 times turn over rate per hour are required.

    b. Aquarium gravel improves the aesthetics of the aquarium.

    c. An aquarium hood keeps dust, dirt and unwanted materials out of the tank.

    d. Each type of tropical fish has its own ideal water temperature.

Questions 13 - 16 refer to the following passage.

The Civil War

The Civil War began on April 12, 1861. The first shots of the Civil War were fired in Fort Sumter, South Carolina. Note that even though more American lives were lost in the Civil War than in any other war, not one person died on that first day. The war began because eleven Southern states seceded from the Union and tried to start their own government, The Confederate States of America.

Why did the states secede? The issue of slavery was a primary cause of the Civil War. The eleven southern states relied heavily on their slaves to foster their farming and plantation lifestyles. The northern states, many of whom had already abolished slavery, did not feel that the southern states should have slaves. The north wanted to free all the slaves and President Lincoln's goal was to both end slavery and preserve the Union. He had Congress declare war on the Confederacy on April 14, 1862. For four long, blood soaked years, the North and South fought.

From 1861 to mid 1863, it seemed as if the South would win this war. However, on July 1, 1863, an epic three day battle was waged on a field in Gettysburg, Pennsylvania. Gettysburg is remembered for being the bloodiest battle in American history. At the end of the three days, the North turned the tide of the war in their favor. The North then went onto dominate the South for the remainder of the war. Another famous event is General Sherman's "March to The Sea," where he famously led the Union Army through Georgia and the Carolinas, burning and destroying everything in their path.

In 1865, the Union army invaded and captured the Confederate capital of Richmond Virginia. Robert E. Lee, leader of the Confederacy surrendered to General Ulysses S. Grant, leader of the Union forces, on April 9, 1865. The Civil War was over and the Union was preserved.

13. What does secede mean?

    a. To break away from

    b. To accomplish

    c. To join

    d. To lose

14. Which of the following statements summarizes a FACT from the passage?

    a. Congress declared war and then the Battle of Fort Sumter began.

    b. Congress declared war after shots were fired at Fort Sumter.

    c. President Lincoln was pro slavery

    d. President Lincoln was at Fort Sumter with Congress

15. Which event finally led the Confederacy to surrender?

    a. The battle of Gettysburg

    b. The battle of Bull Run

    c. The invasion of the confederate capital of Richmond

    d. Sherman's March to the Sea

16. What does the word abolish as used in this passage mean?

    a. To ban

    b. To polish

    c. To support

    d. To destroy

Answer Key

1. A
We know that an annex is like an attic because the text states the annex was above Otto Frank's building.

Choice B is incorrect because an office building doesn't have bedrooms. Choice C is incorrect because a basement would be below the office building. Choice D is incorrect because there would not be a kitchen in an office building.

2. B
The diary has been published in 55 languages so people all over the world can learn about Anne. That is why the passage says it has been continuously in print.

Choice A is incorrect because it is too vague. Choice C is incorrect because it was published after Anne died and she did not write in all three languages. Choice D is incorrect because the passage does not give us any information about what languages Otto Frank spoke.

3. C
Use the process of elimination to figure this out.

Choice A cannot be the correct answer because, otherwise the passage would have simply said that Anne and Margot both died of starvation. Choices B and D cannot be correct because, if the Germans had done something specifically to murder Anne, the passage would have stated that directly. By the process of elimination, choice C has to be the correct answer.

4. D
We can figure this out using context clues. The paragraph is talking about Anne's diary and so, outlet in this instance is a place where Anne can pour her feelings.

Choice A is incorrect answer. That is the literal meaning of the word outlet and the passage is using the figurative meaning. Choice B is incorrect because that is the secondary literal meaning of the word outlet, as in an outlet mall. Again, we are looking for figurative meaning. Choice C is incorrect because there are no clues in the text to support that answer.

5. B
When someone is avid about something that means they are highly interested in the subject. The context clues are dull and boring, because they define the opposite of avid.

6. A
The author is using a simile to compare the books to medicine. Medicine is what you take when you want to feel better. They are suggesting that if you want to feel good, they should read Dr. Seuss' books.

Choice B is incorrect because there is no mention of a doctor's office. Choice C is incorrect because it is using the literal meaning of medicine and the author is using medicine in a figurative way. Choice D is incorrect because it makes no sense. We know not to eat books.

7. D
The publisher is described as intelligent because he knew to get in touch with a famous author to develop a book that children would be interested in reading.

Choice A is incorrect because we can assume that all book publishers must know how to read. Choice B is incorrect because it says in the article that more than one publisher was concerned whether children liked to read. Choice D is incorrect because there is no mention in the article about how well The Cat in the Hat sold when it was first published.

8. B
The passage describes in detail how Dr. Seuss had a great effect on the lives of children through his writing. It names several of his books, tells how he helped children become avid readers and explains his style of writing.

Choice A is incorrect because that is just one single fact about the passage. Choice C is incorrect because that is just one single fact about the passage. Choice D is incorrect because that is just one single fact about the passage. Again, choice B is correct because it encompasses ALL the facts in the passage, not just one single fact.

9. B
The general tone is informal.

10. B
The statement, "Fewer people have aquariums in their office than at home," cannot be inferred from this article.

11. C
The author does not provide evidence for this statement.

12. B
The following statement is an opinion, " Aquarium gravel improves the aesthetics of the aquarium."

13. A
Secede means to break away from because the 11 states wanted to leave the United States and form their own country.

Choice B is incorrect because the states were not accomplishing anything. Choice C is incorrect because the states were trying to leave the USA not join it. Choice D is incorrect because the states seceded before they lost the war.

14. B
Look at the dates in the passage. The shots were fired on April 12 and Congress declared war on April 14.

Choice C is incorrect because the passage states that Lincoln was against slavery. Choice D is incorrect because it never mentions who was or was not at Fort Sumter.

15. C
The passage states that Lee surrendered to Grant after the capture of the capital of the Confederacy, which is Richmond.

Choice A is incorrect because the war continued for 2 years after Gettysburg. Choice B is incorrect because that battle is not mentioned in the passage. Choice D is incorrect because the capture of the capital occurred after the march to the sea.

16. A

When the passage said that the North had *abolished* slavery, it implies that slaves were no longer allowed in the North. In essence slavery was banned.

Choice B makes no sense relative to the context of the passage. Choice C is incorrect because we know the North was fighting slavery, not for it. Choice D is incorrect because slavery is not a tangible thing that can be destroyed. It is a practice that had to be outlawed or banned.

Help with Reading Comprehension

At first sight, reading comprehension tests look challenging especially if you are given long essays to answer only two to three questions. While reading, you might notice your attention waning, or feeling sleepy. Do not be discouraged because there are various tactics and long range strategies that make comprehending even long, boring essays easier.

Your friends before your foes. It is always best to start with essays or passages with familiar subjects rather than those with unfamiliar ones. This approach applies the same logic as tackling easy questions before hard ones. Skip passages that do not interest you and leave them for later.

Don't use 'special' reading techniques. This is not the time for speed-reading or anything like that – just plain ordinary reading – not too slow and not too fast.

Read through the entire passage and the questions before you do anything. Many students try reading the questions first and then looking for answers in the passage thinking this approach is more efficient. What these students do not realize is that it is often hard to navigate in unfamiliar roads. If you do not familiarize yourself with the passage first, looking for answers become not only time-consuming but also dangerous because you might miss the context of the answer you are looking for. If you read the questions first you will only confuse yourself and lose valuable time.

Familiarize yourself with reading comprehension questions. If you are familiar with the common types of reading comprehension questions, you are able to take note of important parts of the passage, saving time. There are six major kinds of reading comprehension questions.

- **Main Idea**- Questions that ask for the central thought or significance of the passage.

- **Specific Details** - Questions that asks for explicitly stated ideas.

- **Drawing Inferences** - Questions that ask for a statement's intended meaning.

- **Tone or Attitude** - Questions that test your ability to sense the emotional state of the author.

- **Context Meaning** – Questions that ask for the meaning of a word depending on the context.

- **Technique** – Questions that ask for the method of organization or the writing style of the author.

Read. Read. Read. The best preparation for reading comprehension tests is always to read, read and read. If you are not used to reading lengthy passages, you will probably lose concentration. Increase your attention span by making a habit out of reading.

Reading Comprehension tests become less daunting when you have trained yourself to read and understand fast. Always remember that it is easier to understand passages you are interested in. Do not read through passages hastily. Make mental notes of ideas you may be asked.

Reading Comprehension Strategy

When facing the reading comprehension section of a standardized test, you need a strategy to be successful. You want to keep several steps in mind:

- First, make a note of the time and the number of sections. Time your work accordingly. Typically, four to five minutes per section is sufficient. Second, read the directions for each selection thoroughly before beginning (and listen well to any additional verbal instructions, as they will often clarify obscure or confusing written guidelines). You must know exactly how to do what you're about to do!

- Now you're ready to begin reading the selection. Read the passage carefully, noting significant characters or events on a scratch sheet of paper or underlining on the test sheet. Many students find making a basic list in the margins helpful. Quickly jot down or underline one-word summaries of characters, notable happenings, numbers, or key ideas. This will help you better retain information and focus wandering thoughts. Remember, however, that your main goal in doing this is to find the information that answers the questions. Even if you find the passage interesting, remember your goal and work fast but stay on track.

- Now read the question and all the choices. Now you have read the passage, have a general idea of the main ideas, and have marked the important points. Read the question and all the choices. Never choose an answer without reading them all! Questions are often designed to confuse – stay focussed and clear. Usually the answer choices will focus on one or two facts or inferences from the passage. Keep these clear in your mind.

- Search for the answer. With a very general idea of what the different choices are, go back to the passage and scan for the relevant information. Watch for big words, unusual or unique words. These make your job easier as you can scan the text for the particular word.

- Mark the Answer. Now you have the key information that the question is looking for. Go back to the question, quickly scan the choices and mark the correct one.

Understand and practice the different types of standardized reading comprehension tests. See the list above for the different types. Typically, there will be several questions dealing with facts from the selection, a couple more inference questions dealing with logical consequences of those facts, and periodically an application-oriented question surfaces to force you to make connections with what you already know. Some students prefer to answer the questions as listed, and feel classifying the question and then ordering is wasting precious time. Other students prefer to answer the different types of questions in order of how easy or difficult they are. The choice is yours and do whatever works for you. If you want to try answering in order of difficulty, here is a recommended order, answer fact questions first; they're easily found within the passage. Tackle inference problems next, after re-reading the question(s) as many times as you need to. Application or 'best guess' questions usually take the longest, so, save them for last.

Use the practice tests to try out both ways of answering and see what works for you.

For more help with reading comprehension, see Multiple Choice Secrets at www.multiple-choice.ca.

Main Idea and Supporting Details

Identifying the main idea, topic and supporting details in a passage can feel like an overwhelming task. The passages used for standardized tests can be boring and seem difficult - Test writers don't use interesting passages or ones that talk about things most people are familiar with. Despite these obstacles, all passages and paragraphs will have the information you need to answer the questions.

The topic of a passage or paragraph is its subject. It's the general idea and can be summed up in a word or short phrase. On some standardized tests, there is a short description of the passage if it's taken from a longer work. Make sure you read the description as it might state the topic of the passage. If not, read the passage and ask yourself, "Who or what is this about?" For example:

> Over the years, school uniforms have been hotly debated. Arguments are made that students have the right to show individuality and express themselves by choosing their own clothes. However, this brings up social and academic issues. Some kids cannot afford to wear the clothes they like and might be bullied by the "better dressed" students. With attention drawn to clothes and the individual, students will lose focus on class work and the reason they are in school. School uniforms should be mandatory.

Ask: What is this paragraph about?

Topic: school uniforms

Once you have the topic, it's easier to find the main idea. The main idea is a specific statement telling what the writer wants you to understand about the topic. Writers usually state the main idea as a thesis statement. If you're looking for the main idea of a single paragraph, the main idea is called the topic sentence and will probably be the first or last sentence. If you're looking for the main idea of an entire passage, look for the thesis statement in either the first or last paragraph. The main idea is usually restated in the conclusion. To find the main idea of a passage or paragraph, follow these steps:

> 1. Find the topic.
>
> 2. Ask yourself, "What point is the author trying to make about the topic?"

3. Create your own sentence summarizing the author's point.

4. Look in the text for the sentence closest in meaning to yours.

Look at the example paragraph again. It's already established that the topic of the paragraph is school uniforms. What is the main idea/topic sentence?

Ask: "What point is the author trying to make about school uniforms?"

Summary: Students should wear school uniforms.

Topic sentence: School uniforms should be mandatory.

Main Idea: School uniforms should be mandatory.

Each paragraph offers supporting details to explain the main idea. The details could be facts or reasons, but they will always answer a question about the main idea. What? Where? Why? When? How? How much/many? Look at the example paragraph again. You'll notice that more than one sentence answers a question about the main idea. These are the supporting details.

Main Idea: School uniforms should be mandatory.

Ask: Why? Some kids cannot afford to wear clothes they like and could be bullied by the "better dressed" kids. Supporting Detail

With attention drawn to clothes and the individual, Students will lose focus on class work and the reason they are in school. Supporting Detail

What if the author doesn't state the main idea in a topic sentence? The passage will have an implied main idea. It's not as difficult to find as it might seem. Paragraphs are always organized around ideas. To find an implied main idea, you need to know the topic and then find the relationship between the supporting details. Ask yourself, "What is the point the author is making about the relationship between the details?"

> Cocoa is what makes chocolate good for you. Chocolate comes in many varieties. These delectable flavors include milk chocolate, dark chocolate, semi-sweet, and white chocolate.

Ask: What is this paragraph about?

Topic: Chocolate

Ask: What? Where? Why? When? How? How much/many?

Supporting details: Chocolate is good for you because it is made of cocoa, Chocolate is delicious, Chocolate comes in different delicious flavors

Ask: What is the relationship between the details and what is the author's point?

Main Idea: Chocolate is good because it is healthy and it tastes good.

Testing Tips for Main Idea Questions

1. **Skim the questions** – not the answer choices - before reading the passage.

2. **Questions about main idea might use the words "theme," "generalization," or "purpose."**

3. **Save questions about the main idea for last.** Questions can often be found in order in the passage.

3. **Underline topic sentences in the passage.** Most tests allow you to write in your test booklet.

4. **Answer the question in your own words before looking at the answer choices.** Then match your answer with an answer choice.

5. **Cross out incorrect answer choices immediately to prevent confusion.**

6. **If two of the answer choices mean the same thing but use different words, they are BOTH incorrect.**

7. **If a question asks about the whole passage, cross out the answer choices that apply only to part of it.**

8. **If only part of the information is correct, that answer choice is incorrect.**

9. **An answer choice that is too broad is incorrect.** All information needs to be backed up by the passage.

10. **Answer choices with extreme wording are usually incorrect.**

Drawing Inferences And Conclusions

Drawing inferences and making conclusions happens all the time. In fact, you probably do it every time you read—sometimes without even realizing it! For example, remember the first time you saw the movie "The Lion King." When you meet Scar for the first time, he is trapping a helpless mouse with his sharp claws preparing to eat it. When you see this action you guess that Scar is going to be a bad character in the movie. Nothing appeared to tell you this. No caption came across the bottom of the screen that said "Bad Guy." No red arrow pointed to Scar and said "Evil Lion." No, you made an inference about his character based on the context clue you were given. You do the same thing when you read!

When you draw an inference or make a conclusion you are doing the same thing, you are making an educated guess based on the hints the author gives you. We call these hints "context clues." Scar trapping the innocent mouse is the context clue about Scar's character.

Usually you are making inferences and drawing conclusions the entire time that you are reading. Whether you realize it or not, you are constantly making educated guesses based on context clues. Think about a time you were reading a book and something happens that you were expecting to happen. You're not psychic! Actually, you were picking up on the context clues and making inferences about what was going to happen next!

Let's try an easy example. Read the following sentences and answer the questions at the end of the passage.

Shelly really likes to help people. She loves her job because she gets to help people every single day. However, Shelly has to work long hours and she can get called in the middle of the night for emergencies. She wears a white lab coat at work and usually she carries a stethoscope.

What is most likely Shelly's job?

    a. Musician

    b. Lawyer

    c. Doctor

    d. Teacher

This probably seemed easy. Drawing inferences isn't always this simple, but it is the same basic principle. How did you know Shelly was a doctor? She helps people, she works long hours, she wears a white lab coat, and she gets called in for emergencies at night. Context Clues! Nowhere in the paragraph did it say Shelly was a doctor, but you were able to draw that conclusion based on the information provided in the paragraph. This is how it's done!

There is a catch, though. Remember that when you draw inferences based on reading, you should only use the information given to you by the author. Sometimes it is easy for us to make conclusions based on knowledge that is already in our mind—but that can lead you to drawing an incorrect inference. For example, let's pretend there is a bully at your school named Brent. Now let's say you read a story and the main character's name is Brent. You could NOT infer that the character in the story is a bully just because his name is Brent. You should only use the information given to you by the author to avoid drawing the wrong conclusion.

Let's try another example. Read the passage below and answer the question.

Social media is an extremely popular new form of connecting and communicating over the internet. Since Facebook's original launch in 2004, millions of people have joined in the social media craze. In fact, it is estimated that almost 75% of all internet users aged 18 and older use some form of social media. Facebook started at Harvard University as a way to get students connected. However, it quickly grew into a worldwide phenomenon and today, the founder of Facebook, Mark Zuckerberg has an estimated net worth of 28.5 billion dollars.

Facebook is not the only social media platform, though. Other sites such as Twitter, Instagram, and Snapchat have since been invented and are quickly becoming just as popular! Many social media users actually use more than one type of social media. Furthermore, most social media sites have created mobile apps that allow people to connect via social media virtually anywhere in the world!

What is the most likely reason that other social media sites like Twitter and Instagram were created?

    a. Professors at Harvard University made it a class project.

    b. Facebook was extremely popular and other people thought they could also be successful by designing social media sites.

    c. Facebook was not connecting enough people.

    d. Mark Zuckerberg paid people to invent new social media sites because he wanted lots of competition.

Here, the correct answer is B. Facebook was extremely popular and other people thought they could also be successful by designing social media sites. How do we know this? What are the context clues? Take a look at the first paragraph. What do we know based on this paragraph? Well, one sentence refers to Facebook's original launch. This suggests that Facebook was one of the first social media sites. In addition, we know that the founder of Facebook has been extremely successful and is worth billions of dollars. From this we can infer that other people wanted to imitate Facebook's idea and become just as successful as Mark Zuckerberg.

Let's go through the other answers. If you chose A, it might be because Facebook started at Harvard University, so you drew the conclusion that all other social media sites were also started at Harvard University. However, there is no mention of class projects, professors, or students designing social media. So there doesn't seem to be enough support for choice A.

If you chose C, you might have been drawing your own conclusions based on outside information. Maybe none of your friends are on Facebook, so you made an inference that Facebook didn't connect enough people, so more sites were invented. Or maybe you think the people who connect on Facebook are too old, so you don't think Facebook connects enough people your age. This might be true, but remember inferences should be drawn from the information the author gives you!

If you chose D, you might be using the information that Mark Zuckerberg is worth over 28 billion dollars. It would be easy for him to pay others to design new sites, but remember, you need to use context clues! He is very wealthy, but that statement was giving you information about how successful Facebook was—not suggesting that he paid others to design more sites!

So remember, drawing inferences and conclusions is simply about using the information you are given to make an educated guess. You do this every single day so don't let this concept scare you. Look for the context clues, make sure they support your claim, and you'll be able to make accurate inferences and conclusions!

Vocabulary

THIS SECTION CONTAINS A SELF-ASSESSMENT AND VOCABULARY TUTORIAL. The tutorial is designed to familiarize with general principles. So, while the self-assessment contains general questions similar to the Vocabulary questions likely to be on the Nelson Denny exam, but are not intended to be identical to the exam questions. The tutorials are not designed to be a complete Vocabulary course, and it is assumed that students have some familiarity with Vocabulary questions. If you do not understand parts of the tutorial, or find the tutorial difficult, it is recommended that you seek out additional instruction.

Note that these questions are for skill practice only. The questions below are not the same as you will find on the Nelson Denny - that would be too easy! And nobody knows what the questions will be and they change all the time. Mostly the changes consist of substituting new questions for old, but the changes can be new question formats or styles, changes to the number of questions in each section, changes to the time limits for each section and combining sections. Below are general Vocabulary questions that cover the same areas as the Nelson Denny. So, while the format and exact wording of the questions may differ slightly, and change from year to year, if you can answer the questions below, you will have no problem with the Vocabulary section of the Nelson Denny.

Vocabulary Self-Assessment

The purpose of the self-assessment is:

- Identify your strengths and weaknesses.
- Develop your personalized study plan (above)
- Get accustomed to the Nelson Denny format
- Extra practice – the self-assessments are almost a full 3rd practice test!
- Provide a baseline score for preparing your study schedule.

Since this is a self-assessment, and depending on how confident you are with Vocabulary, timing is optional. The self-assessment has 14 questions, so allow about 15 minutes to complete this assessment.

Once complete, use the table below to assess your understanding of the content, and prepare your study schedule described in chapter 1.

80% - 100%	Excellent – you have mastered the content!
60 – 79%	Good. You have a working knowledge. Even though you can just pass this section, you may want to review the Tutorials and do some extra practice to see if you can improve your mark.
40% - 59%	Below Average. You do not understand Vocabulary problems. Review the tutorials, and retake this quiz again in a few days, before proceeding to the rest of the study guide.
Less than 40%	Poor. You have a very limited understanding of Vocabulary problems. Please review the Tutorials, and retake this quiz again in a few days, before proceeding to the rest of the study guide.

Answer Sheet

	A	B	C	D
1	○	○	○	○
2	○	○	○	○
3	○	○	○	○
4	○	○	○	○
5	○	○	○	○
6	○	○	○	○
7	○	○	○	○
8	○	○	○	○
9	○	○	○	○
10	○	○	○	○
11	○	○	○	○
12	○	○	○	○
13	○	○	○	○
14	○	○	○	○
15	○	○	○	○
16	○	○	○	○
17	○	○	○	○
18	○	○	○	○
19	○	○	○	○
20	○	○	○	○

Vocabulary Self-Assessment

Choose the word that best suits the given definition.

1. **ADJECTIVE** Corrupted, Impure.
   a. Adulterate
   b. Harbor
   c. Infuriate
   d. Inculcate

2. **NOUN** Eagerness and enthusiasm.
   a. Alacrity
   b. Happiness
   c. Donator
   d. Marital

3. **VERB** To make less severe.
   a. Suspense
   b. Alleviate
   c. Ingrate
   d. Action

4. **VERB** To make blissful or happy.
   a. Brand
   b. Negate
   c. Beatify
   d. Train

5. **NOUN** One who gives a gift or who gives money to a charity organization.
   a. Captain
   b. Benefactor
   c. Source
   d. Teacher

6. **ADJECTIVE** Hidden, secret, disguised.
   a. Accustomed
   b. Covert
   c. Hide
   d. Carriage

7. **VERB** Straightforward, open and sincere.
   a. Lawful
   b. Candid
   c. True
   d. Lawful

8. **VERB** Fearless or invulnerable to intimidation and fear.
   a. Feeble
   b. Strongest
   c. Dauntless
   d. Super

9. **VERB** To remove a leader or high official from position.
   a. Sack
   b. Suspend
   c. Depose
   d. Dropped

Vocabulary

10. VERB To build up or strengthen relative to morals or religion.

   a. Sanctify
   b. Amplify
   c. Edify
   d. Wry

Choose the best definition of the given word.

11. Choose the best definition for virago.

   a. Loud and domineering woman
   b. A quiet woman
   c. A load domineering Man
   d. A quiet man

12. Choose the best definition of deprecate.

   a. Approve
   b. Indifference
   c. Disapprove
   d. None of the above

13. Choose the best definition for succor.

   a. To suck on
   b. To hate
   c. To like
   d. Give help of assistance

14. Choose the best definition of specious.

   a. Logical
   b. Illogical
   c. Emotional
   d. 2 species

15. Choose the best definition of proscribe.

   a. Welcome
   b. Write a prescription
   c. Banish
   d. Give a diagnosis

16. Choose the best definition of pernicious.

   a. Deadly
   b. Infectious
   c. Common
   d. Rare

17. Choose the best definition of pedestrian.

   a. Rare
   b. Often
   c. Walking or Running
   d. Commonplace

18. Choose the best definition of petulant.

   a. Patient
   b. Childish
   c. Impatient
   d. Mature

19. Choose the best definition of stint.

   a. Thrifty
   b. Annoyed
   c. Dislike
   d. Insult

20. Choose the best definition of precipitate.

   a. To rain
   b. To throw down
   c. To throw up
   d. To snow

Answer Key

1. A
Adulterate VERB corrupted; impure; adulterated.

2. A
Alacrity NOUN eagerness; liveliness; enthusiasm.

3. B
Alleviate VERB to make less severe, as a pain or difficulty.

4. C
Beatify VERB to make blissful.

5. B
Benefactor NOUN somebody who gives one a gift. Usually refers to someone who gives money to a charity or another form of organization.

6. B
Covert ADJECTIVE Partially hidden, disguised, secret, surreptitious.

7. B
Candid ADJECTIVE straightforward, open and sincere.

8. C
Dauntless ADJECTIVE invulnerable to fear or intimidation.

9. C
Depose VERB to remove (a leader) from (high) office, without killing the incumbent.

10. C
Edify VERB to instruct or improve morally or intellectually.

11. A
Virago NOUN given to undue belligerence or ill manner at the slightest provocation; a shrew.

12. C
Deprecate VERB to belittle or express disapproval of.

13. D
Succor NOUN aid, assistance or relief given to one in distress; ministration.

14. B
Specious ADJECTIVE seemingly well-reasoned or factual, but actually fallacious or insincere; strongly held but false.

15. C
Proscribe ADJECTIVE seemingly well-reasoned or factual, but actually fallacious or insincere; strongly held but false.

16. A
Pernicious ADJECTIVE causing much harm in a subtle way.

17. D
Pedestrian ADJECTIVE ordinary, dull; everyday; unexceptional.

18. C
Petulant ADJECTIVE childishly irritable, impatient.

19. A
Stint VERB to be sparing, thrifty.

20. A
Precipitate VERB to have water in the air fall to the ground, for example as rain, snow, sleet.

Nelson Denny Practice Test Questions

Practice Test Questions Set I

THE PRACTICE TEST QUESTIONS PORTION PRESENTS QUESTIONS REPRESENTATIVE OF WHAT YOU CAN EXPECT TO FIND ON THE NELSON DENNY. However, they are not intended to match exactly what is on the NDRT.

For the best results, take the practice test questions as if it were the real exam. Set aside time when you will not be disturbed, and a location that is quiet and free of distractions. Read the instructions carefully, read each question carefully, and answer to the best of your ability.

Use the bubble answer sheets provided. When you have completed the practice questions, check your answer against the Answer Key and read the explanation provided.

Reading Comprehension Answer Sheet

1. A B C D   11. A B C D   21. A B C D
2. A B C D   12. A B C D   22. A B C D
3. A B C D   13. A B C D   23. A B C D
4. A B C D   14. A B C D   24. A B C D
5. A B C D   15. A B C D   25. A B C D
6. A B C D   16. A B C D   26. A B C D
7. A B C D   17. A B C D   27. A B C D
8. A B C D   18. A B C D   28. A B C D
9. A B C D   19. A B C D   29. A B C D
10. A B C D   20. A B C D   30. A B C D

Practice Test Questions Set I Vocabulary Answer Sheet

1. A B C D
2. A B C D
3. A B C D
4. A B C D
5. A B C D
6. A B C D
7. A B C D
8. A B C D
9. A B C D
10. A B C D
11. A B C D
12. A B C D
13. A B C D
14. A B C D
15. A B C D
16. A B C D
17. A B C D
18. A B C D
19. A B C D
20. A B C D
21. A B C D
22. A B C D
23. A B C D
24. A B C D
25. A B C D
26. A B C D
27. A B C D
28. A B C D
29. A B C D
30. A B C D
31. A B C D
32. A B C D
33. A B C D
34. A B C D
35. A B C D
36. A B C D
37. A B C D
38. A B C D
39. A B C D
40. A B C D
41. A B C D
42. A B C D
43. A B C D
44. A B C D
45. A B C D
46. A B C D
47. A B C D
48. A B C D
49. A B C D
50. A B C D
51. A B C D
52. A B C D
53. A B C D
54. A B C D
55. A B C D
56. A B C D
57. A B C D
58. A B C D
59. A B C D
60. A B C D
61. A B C D
62. A B C D
63. A B C D
64. A B C D
65. A B C D
66. A B C D
67. A B C D
68. A B C D
69. A B C D
70. A B C D
71. A B C D
72. A B C D
73. A B C D
74. A B C D
75. A B C D
76. A B C D
77. A B C D
78. A B C D
79. A B C D
80. A B C D

Directions: The following questions are based on several reading passages. Each passage is followed by a series of questions. Read each passage carefully, and then answer the questions based on it. You may reread the passage as often as you wish. When you have finished answering the questions based on one passage, go right onto the next passage. Choose the best answer based on the information given and implied.

Questions 1 – 4 refer to the following passage.

Passage 1 - The Life of Helen Keller

Many people have heard of Helen Keller. She is famous because she was unable to see or hear, but learned to speak and read and went onto attend college and earn a degree. Her life is a very interesting story, one that she developed into an autobiography, which was then adapted into both a stage play and a movie. How did Helen Keller overcome her disabilities to become a famous woman? Read on to find out.

Helen Keller was not born blind and deaf. When she was a small baby, she had a very high fever for several days. As a result of her sudden illness, baby Helen lost her eyesight and her hearing. Because she was so young when she went deaf and blind, Helen Keller never had any recollection of being able to see or hear. Since she could not hear, she could not learn to talk. Since she could not see, it was difficult for her to move around. For the first six years of her life, her world was very still and dark.

Imagine what Helen's childhood was like. She could not hear her mother's voice. She could not see the beauty of her parent's farm. She could not recognize who was giving her a hug, or a bath or even where her bedroom was each night. Worse, she could not communicate with her parents in any way. She could not express her feelings or tell them the things she wanted. It must have been a very sad childhood.

When Helen was six years old, her parents hired her a teacher named Anne Sullivan. Anne was a young woman who was almost blind. However, she could hear and she could read Braille, so she was a perfect teacher for young Helen. At first, Anne had a very hard time teaching Helen anything. She described her first impression of Helen as a "wild thing, not a child." Helen did not like Anne at first either. She bit and hit Anne when Anne tried to teach her. However, the two of them eventually came to have a great deal of love and respect.

Anne taught Helen to hear by putting her hands on people's throats. She could feel the sounds people made. In time, Helen learned to feel what people said. Next, Anne taught Helen to read Braille, which is a way that books are written for the blind. Finally, Anne taught Helen to talk. Although Helen did learn to talk, it was hard for anyone but Anne to understand her.

As Helen grew older, she amazed more and more people with her story. She went to college and wrote books about her life. She gave talks to the public, with Anne at her side, translating her words. Today, both Anne Sullivan and Helen Keller are famous women who are respected for their lives' work.

1. Helen Keller could not see and hear and so, what was her biggest problem in childhood?

    a. Inability to communicate

    b. Inability to walk

    c. Inability to play

    d. Inability to eat

2. Helen learned to hear by feeling the vibrations people made when they spoke. What were these vibrations were felt through?

    a. Mouth

    b. Throat

    c. Ears

    d. Lips

3. From the passage, we can infer that Anne Sullivan was a patient teacher. We can infer this because

    a. Helen hit and bit her and Anne remained her teacher.

    b. Anne taught Helen to read only.

    c. Anne was hard of hearing too.

    d. Anne wanted to be a teacher.

4. Helen Keller learned to speak but Anne translated her words when she spoke in public. The reason Helen needed a translator was because

    a. Helen spoke another language.

    b. Helen's words were hard for people to understand.

    c. Helen spoke very quietly.

    d. Helen did not speak but only used sign language.

Questions 5 – 8 refer to the following passage.

Passage 2 - Ways Characters Communicate in Theater

Playwrights give their characters voices in a way that gives depth and added meaning to what happens on stage during their play. There are different types of speech in scripts that allow characters to talk with themselves, with other characters, and even with the audience.

It is very unique to theater that characters may talk "to themselves." When characters do this, the speech they give is called a soliloquy. Soliloquies are usually poetic, introspective, moving, and can tell audience members about the feelings, motivations, or suspicions of an individual character without that character having to reveal them to other characters on stage. "To be or not to be" is a famous soliloquy given by Hamlet as he considers difficult but important themes, such as life and death.

The most common type of communication in plays is when one character is speaking to another or a group of other characters. This is generally called dialogue, but can also be called monologue if one character speaks without being interrupted for a long time. It is not necessarily the most important type of communication, but it is the most common because the plot of the play cannot really progress without it.

Lastly, and most unique to theater (although it has been used somewhat in film) is when a character speaks directly to the audience. This is called an aside, and scripts usually specifically direct actors to do this. Asides are usually comical, an inside joke between the character and the audience, and very short. The actor will usually face the audience when delivering them, even if it's for a moment, so the audience can recognize this move as an aside.

All three of these types of communication are important to the art of theater, and have been perfected by famous playwrights like Shakespeare. Understanding these types of communication can help an audience member grasp what is artful about the script and action of a play.

5. According to the passage, characters in plays communicate to

      a. move the plot forward

      b. show the private thoughts and feelings of one character

      c. make the audience laugh

      d. add beauty and artistry to the play

6. When Hamlet delivers "To be or not to be," he can be described as

a. solitary
b. thoughtful
c. dramatic
d. hopeless

7. The author uses parentheses to punctuate "although it has been used somewhat in film,"

a. to show that films are less important
b. instead of using commas so that the sentence is not interrupted
c. because parenthesis help separate details that are not as important
d. to show that films are not as artistic

Questions 9 – 11 refer to the following passage.

Passage 3 - Low Blood Sugar

As the name suggest, low blood sugar is low sugar levels in the bloodstream. This can occur when you have not eaten properly and undertake strenuous activity, or, when you are very hungry. When Low blood sugar occurs regularly and is ongoing, it is a medical condition called hypoglycaemia. This condition can occur in diabetics and in healthy adults.

Causes of low blood sugar can include excessive alcohol consumption, metabolic problems, stomach surgery, pancreas, liver or kidneys problems, as well as a side-effect of some medications.

Symptoms

There are different symptoms depending on the severity of the case.

Mild hypoglycaemia can lead to feelings of nausea and hunger. The patient may also feel nervous, jittery and have fast heart beats. Sweaty skin, clammy and cold skin are likely symptoms.
Moderate hypoglycaemia can result in a short temper, confusion, nervousness, fear and blurring of vision. The patient may feel weak and unsteady.

Severe cases of hypo glycaemia can lead to seizures, coma, fainting spells, nightmares, headaches, excessive sweats and severe tiredness.

Diagnosis of low blood sugar

A doctor can diagnosis this medical condition by asking the patient questions and testing blood and urine samples. Home testing kits are available for patients to monitor blood sugar levels. It is important to see a qualified doctor though. A doctor can test to safely rule out other medical conditions that could affect blood sugar levels.

Treatment

Quick treatments include drinking or eating foods and drinks with high sugar contents. Good examples include soda, fruit juice, hard candy and raisins. Glucose energy tablets can also help. Doctors may also recommend medications and well as changes in diet and exercise routine to treat chronic low blood sugar.

8. Based on the article, which of the following is true?

    a. Low blood sugar can happen to anyone.

    b. Low blood sugar only happens to diabetics.

    c. Low blood sugar can occur even.

    d. None of the statements are true.

9. Which of the following are the author's opinion?

    a. Quick treatments include drinking or eating foods and drinks with high sugar contents.

    b. None of the statements are opinions.

    c. This condition can occur in diabetics and in healthy adults.

    d. There are different symptoms depending on the severity of the case

10. What is the author's purpose?

    a. To inform

    b. To persuade

    c. To entertain

    d. To analyze

11. Which of the following is not a detail?

    a. A doctor can diagnosis this medical condition by asking the patient questions and testing.

    b. A doctor will test blood and urine samples.

    c. Glucose energy tablets can also help.

    d. Home test kits monitor blood sugar levels.

Questions 12 – 14 refer to the following passage.

How To Get A Good Nights Sleep

Sleep is just as essential for healthy living as water, air and food. Sleep allows the body to rest and replenish depleted energy levels. Sometimes we may for various reasons have trouble sleeping which has a serious effect on our health. Those who have prolonged sleeping problems are facing a serious medical condition and should see a qualified doctor when possible for help. Here is simple guide that can help you sleep better at night.

Try to create a natural pattern of waking up and sleeping around the same time every day - avoid going to bed too early and sleeping past your usual wake up time. Going to bed and getting up at radically different times everyday confuses your body clock. Try to establish a natural rhythm as much as you can.

Exercises and a bit of physical activity can help you sleep better at night. If you are having problem sleeping, try to be as active as you can during the day. If you are tired from physical activity, falling asleep is a natural and easy process
for your body. If you remain inactive during the day, you will find it harder to sleep properly at night. Try walking, jogging, swimming or simple stretches close to your bed time.

Afternoon naps are great to refresh you during the day, but they may also keep you awake at night. If you feel sleepy during the day, get up, take a walk and get busy to keep from sleeping. Stretching is a good way to increase blood flow to the brain and keep you alert so that you don't sleep during the day. This will help you sleep better night.

> A warm bath or a glass of milk in the evening can help your body relax and prepare for sleep. A cold bath will wake you up and keep you up for several hours. Also avoid eating too late before bed.

12. How would you describe this sentence?

    a. A recommendation
    b. An opinion
    c. A fact
    d. A diagnosis

13. Which of the following is an alternative title for this article?

a. Exercise and a good night's sleep

b. Benefits of a good night's sleep

c. Tips for a good night's sleep

d. Lack of sleep is a serious medical condition

14. Which of the following cannot be inferred from this article?

a. Biking is helpful for getting a good night's sleep

b. Mental activity is helpful for getting a good night's sleep

c. Eating bedtime snacks is not recommended

d. Getting up at the same time is helpful for a good night's sleep

15. What is a disadvantage of taking naps?

a. They may keep you awake.

b. There are no disadvantages

c. They may help you sleep better

d. They may affect your diet

Question 16 refers to the following Table of Contents.

Contents

Contents

    Science Self-assessment 81
    Answer Key 91
    Science Tutorials 96
    Scientific Method 96
    Biology 99
    Heredity: Genes and Mutation 104
    Classification 108
    Ecology 110
    Chemistry 112
    Energy: Kinetic and Mechanical 126
    Energy: Work and Power 130
    Force: Newton's Three Laws 132

16. Consider the table of contents above. What page would you find information about natural selection and adaptation?

    a. 81
    b. 90
    c. 110
    d. 132

Questions 17 – 19 refer to the following passage.

Passage 5 - Pearl Harbor

In 1941, the world was at war. The United States was trying to stay out of the conflict. In Europe, the countries of Germany and Italy had formed an alliance to expand their land and territory. Germany had already taken over Poland, Denmark, and parts of France. They were heading next toward England and due to all the fighting in Europe, there were battles taking place as far south as North Africa, where the German and Italian armies were fighting the British.

This got even worse when the Asian nation of Japan formed an alliance with Germany and Italy. Together, the three countries called themselves, the AXIS. Now, the war was in the Pacific as well as in Europe and Northern Africa. Many Americans thought that perhaps now was the time for the United States to join with its ally, Great Britain and stop the Axis from taking over more regions of the world.

In 1941, Franklin Roosevelt was President of the United States. His fear at the time was that Japan would try to take over many countries in Asia. He did not want to see that happen, so he moved some of the United States warships that had been stationed in San Diego, to the military base at Pearl Harbor, in Honolulu, Hawaii.

Japan quietly plotted their attack. They waited until the early hours of the morning on Sunday, December 7, 1941. Then, 350 Japanese war plans began to drop bombs on the U.S. ships at Pearl Harbor. The first bombs fell at 7:48 a.m. and only 90 minutes later, the attack was over. Pearl Harbor was decimated. 8 battleships were damaged. Eleven ships were sunk and 300 U.S. planes were destroyed. Most devastating was the loss of life 2,400 U.S. military members was killed in the attack and 1, 282 were injured.

President Roosevelt addressed the country via the radio and said "Today is a day that will live in infamy." He asked Congress to declare war on Japan. War was declared on Japan on December 8th and on Germany and Italy on December 11th. The United States had entered World War Two.

17. After reading the passage, what can you infer infamy means?

a. Famous
b. Remembered in a good way
c. Remembered in a bad way
d. Easily forgotten

18. What three countries formed the Axis?

a. Italy, England, Germany
b. United States, England, Italy
c. Germany, Japan, Italy
d. Germany, Japan, United States

19. What do you think was President Roosevelt's reason for moving warships to Pearl Harbor?

a. He feared Japan would bomb San Diego
b. He knew Japan was going to attack Pearl Harbor
c. He was planning to attack Japan
d. He wanted to try to protect Asian countries from Japanese takeover

20. Why do you think Japan chose a Sunday morning at 7:48 am for their attack?

a. They knew the military slept late
b. There is a law against bombing countries on a Sunday
c. They wanted the attack to catch people by surprise
d. That was the only free time they had to attack.

Questions 21 - 24 refer to the following recipe.

If You Have Allergies, You're Not Alone

People who experience allergies might joke that their immune systems have let them down or are seriously lacking. Truthfully though, people who experience allergic reactions or allergy symptoms during certain times of the year have heightened immune systems that are, "better" than those of people who have perfectly healthy but less militant immune systems.

Still, when a person has an allergic reaction, they are having an adverse reaction to a substance that is considered normal to most people. Mild allergic reactions usually have symptoms like itching, runny nose, red eyes, or bumps or discoloration of the skin. More serious allergic reactions, such as those to animal and insect poisons or certain foods, may result in the closing of the throat, swelling of the eyes, low blood pressure, inability to breath, and can even be fatal.

Different treatments help different allergies, depending on the nature and severity of the allergy. It is recommended to patients with severe allergies to take extra precautions, such as carrying an EpiPen, which treats anaphylactic shock and may prevent death, always in order for the remedy to be readily available and more effective. When an allergy is not so severe, treatments may be used just relieve a person of uncomfortable symptoms. Over the counter allergy medicines treat milder symptoms, and can be bought at any grocery store and used in moderation to help people with allergies live normally.

There are many tests available to assess whether a person has allergies or what they may be allergic to, and advances in these tests and the medicine used to treat patients continues to improve. Despite this fact, allergies still affect many people throughout the year or even every day. Medicines used to treat allergies have side-effects, and it is difficult to bring the body into balance with the use of medicine. Regardless, many of those who live with allergies are grateful for what is available and find it useful in maintaining their lifestyles.

21. According to this passage, which group does the word "militant" belong in

    a. sickly, ailing, faint

    b. strength, power, vigor

    c. active, fighting, warring

    d. worn, tired, breaking down

22. The author says that "medicines used to treat allergies have side-effects of their own" to

    a. point out that doctors aren't very good at diagnosing and treating allergies

    b. argue that because of the large number of people with allergies, a cure will never be found

    c. explain that allergy medicines aren't cures, and some compromise must be made

    d. argue that more wholesome remedies should be researched and medicines banned

23. It can be inferred that _____ recommend that some people with allergies carry medicine with them.

   a. the author

   b. doctors

   c. the makers of EpiPen

   d. people with allergies

24. The author has written this passage to

   a. inform readers on symptoms of allergies so people with allergies can get help

   b. persuade readers to be proud of having allergies

   c. inform readers on different remedies so people with allergies receive the right help

   d. describe different types of allergies, their symptoms, and their remedies

Questions 25 – 26 refer to the following email.

SUBJECT: MEDICAL STAFF CHANGES

To all staff:

This email is to advise you of a paper on recommended medical staff changes has been posted to the Human Resources website.

The contents are of primary interest to medical staff, other staff may be interested in reading it, particularly those in medical support roles.

The paper deals with several major issues:

   1. Improving our ability to attract top quality staff to the hospital, and retain our existing staff. These changes will make our position and departmental names internationally recognizable and comparable with North American and North Asian departments and positions.

   2. Improving our ability to attract top quality staff by introducing greater flexibility in the departmental structure.

   3. General comments on issues to be further discussed relative to research staff.

The changes outlined in this paper are significant. I encourage you to read the document and send to me any comments you may have, so that it can be enhanced and improved.

Gordon Simms
Administrator,
Seven Oaks Regional Hospital

25. Are all hospital staff required to read the document posted to the Human Resources website?

    a. Yes all staff are required to read the document.

    b. No, reading the document is optional.

    c. Only medical staff are required to read the document.

    d. none of the above are correct.

26. Have the changes to medical staff been made?

    a. Yes, the changes have been made.

    b. No, the changes are only being discussed.

    c. Some of the changes have been made.

    d. None of the choices are correct.

Questions 27 – 30 refer to the following passage.

When a Poet Longs to Mourn, He Writes an Elegy

Poems are an expressive, especially emotional, form of writing. They have been in literature virtually from the time civilizations invented the written word. Poets often portrayed as moody, secluded, and even troubled, but this is because poets are introspective and feel deeply about the current events and cultural norms they are surrounded with. Poets often produce the most telling literature, giving insight into the society and mind-set they come from. This can be done in many forms.

The oldest types of poems often include many stanzas, which may or may not rhyme, and are more about telling a story than experimenting with language or words. The most common types of ancient poetry are epics, which are usually extremely long stories that follow a hero through his journey, or ellegies, which are often solemn in tone and used to mourn or lament something or someone. The Mesopotamians are often said to have invented the written word, and their literature is among the oldest in the world, including the epic poem titled "Epic of Gilgamesh." Similar in style and length to "Gilgamesh" is "Beowulf," an ellegy written in Old English and set in Scandinavia. These poems are often used by professors as the earliest examples of literature.

The importance of poetry was revived in the Renaissance. At this time, Europeans discovered the style and beauty of ancient Greek arts, and poetry was among those. Shakespeare is the most well-known poet of the time, and he used poetry not only to write poems but also to write plays for the theater. The most popular forms of poetry during the Renaissance included villanelles, (a nineteen-line poetic form) sonnets, as well as the epic. Poets during this time focused on style and form, and developed very specific rules and outlines for how an exceptional poem should be written.

As often happens in the arts, modern poets have rejected the constricting rules of Renaissance poets, and free form poems are much more popular. Some modern poems would read just like stories if they weren't arranged into lines and stanzas. It is difficult to tell which poems and poets will be the most important, because works of art often become more famous in hindsight, after the poet has died and society can look at itself without being in the moment. Modern poetry continues to develop, and will no doubt continue to change as values, thought, and writing continue to change.

Poems can be among the most enlightening and uplifting texts for a person to read if they are looking to connect with the past, connect with other people, or try to gain an understanding of what is happening in their time.

27. In summary, the author has written this passage

   a. as a foreword that will introduce a poem in a book or magazine

   b. because she loves poetry and wants more people to like it

   c. to give a brief history of poems

   d. to convince students to write poems

28. The author organizes the paragraphs mainly by

   a. moving chronologically, explaining which types of poetry were common in that time

   b. talking about new types of poems each paragraph and explaining them a little

   c. focusing on one poet or group of people and the poems they wrote

   d. explaining older types of poetry so she can talk about modern poetry

29. The author's claim that poetry has been around "virtually from the time civilizations invented the written word" is supported by the detail that

   a. Beowulf is written in Old English, which is not really in use any longer

   b. epic poems told stories about heroes

   c. the Renaissance poets tried to copy Greek poets

   d. the Mesopotamians are credited with both inventing the word and writing "Epic of Gilgamesh"

30. According to the passage, the word "telling" means

   a. speaking

   b. significant

   c. soothing

   d. wordy

Section II - Vocabulary

Choose the word that matches the given definition.

1. VERB To build up or strengthen relative to morals or religion.

    a. Sanctify
    b. Amplify
    c. Edify
    d. Wry

2. NOUN Exit or way out.

    a. Door-jamb
    b. Egress
    c. Regress
    d. Furtherance

3. ADJECTIVE Private, personal.

    a. Confidential
    b. Hysteric
    c. Simplistic
    d. Promissory

4. NOUN Serious criminal offence that is punishable by death or imprisonment above a year.

    a. Trespass
    b. Hampers
    c. Felony
    d. Obligatory

5. VERB To encourage or incite troublesome acts.

    a. Comment
    b. Foment
    c. Integument
    d. Atonement

6. ADJECTIVE Dignified, solemn that is appropriate for a funeral.

    a. Funereal
    b. Prediction
    c. Wailing
    d. Vociferous

7. NOUN Warmth and kindness of disposition.

    a. Seethe
    b. Geniality
    c. Desists
    d. Predicate

8. ADJECTIVE Polite and well mannered.

    a. Chivalrous
    b. Hilarious
    c. Genteel
    d. Governance

9. VERB To encourage, stimulate or incite and provoke.

    a. Push
    b. Force
    c. Threaten
    d. Goad

10. ADJECTIVE Shocking, terrible or wicked.

   a. Pleasantries
   b. Heinous
   c. Shrewd
   d. Provencal

11. NOUN A person of thing that tells or announces the coming of someone or something.

   a. Harbinger
   b. Evasion
   c. Apostate
   d. Coquette

12. ADJECTIVE Similar or identical.

   a. Soluble
   b. Assembly
   c. Conclave
   d. Homologous

13. ADJECTIVE Common, not honorable or noble.

   a. Princely
   b. Ignoble
   c. Shameful
   d. Sham

14. ADJECTIVE Irrelevant not having substance or matter.

   a. Immaterial
   b. Prohibition
   c. Prediction
   d. Brokerage

15. ADJECTIVE Perfect, no faults or errors.

   a. Impeccable
   b. Formidable
   c. Genteel
   d. Disputation

16. VERB Place side by side for contrast or comparison.

   a. Peccadillo
   b. Fallible
   c. Congeal
   d. Juxtapose

17. NOUN Ruling council of a military government.

   a. Sophist
   b. Counsel
   c. Virago
   d. Junta

18. NOUN Someone who takes more time than necessary.

   a. Demagogue
   b. Haggard
   c. Laggard
   d. Investiture

19. ADJECTIVE Lacking enthusiasm, strength or energy.

   a. Hapless
   b. Languid
   c. Ubiquitous
   d. Promiscuous

20. NOUN A person of influence, rank or distinction.

    a. Consummate
    b. Sinister
    c. Accolade
    d. Magnate

21. NOUN A lingering disease or ailment of the human body.

    a. Treatment
    b. Frontal
    c. Malady
    d. Assiduous

22. ADJECTIVE Quick and light in movement.

    a. Quickest
    b. Nimble
    c. Rapacious
    d. Perspicuities

23. ADJECTIVE A loud unpleasant noise.

    a. Nosy
    b. Racket
    c. Ravage
    d. Noisome

24. ADJECTIVE Relating to a wedding or marriage.

    a. Nefarious
    b. Fluctuate
    c. Nuptial
    d. Flatulence

25. ADJECTIVE Open display or apparent.

    a. Ostensible
    b. Complacent
    c. Revealing
    d. Harrowing

26. NOUN A sheet of paper that can be folded into 8 leaves.

    a. Octagon
    b. Harangue
    c. Octavo
    d. Wreckage

27. ADJECTIVE Appearing weak or pale.

    a. Pallid
    b. Palliative
    c. Deviant
    d. Expatiate

28. NOUN A picture or series of pictures representing a continuous scene.

    a. Accolade
    b. Obdurate
    c. Panorama
    d. Personification

29. NOUN A self contradictory statement that can only be true if its false and vice versa.

    a. Inbred
    b. Paradox
    c. Attribute
    d. Fealty

30. ADJECTIVE Often complaining.

   a. Querulous
   b. Complaint
   c. Compound
   d. Vestige

31. NOUN Stillness or pause, something that quiets or represses.

   a. Plausible
   b. Justification
   c. Quietus
   d. Quarantine

32. VERB Question or inquiry.

   a. Cite
   b. Query
   c. Linger
   d. Gibe

33. NOUN A deep narrow valley or gorge cause by running water.

   a. Rumbling
   b. Ravine
   c. Delectable
   d. Distraught

34. VERB Move back or move away.

   a. Implicate
   b. Oscillate
   c. Recede
   d. Meander

35. VERB To become wrinkled.

   a. Sheave
   b. Shrivel
   c. Vernal
   d. Meticulous

36. NOUN A place where people tan hides to make leather.

   a. Shrapnel
   b. Leathery
   c. Tannery
   d. Malleable

37. NOUN An amusing story.

   a. Acronym
   b. Anecdote
   c. Testament
   d. Chaplain

38. ADJECTIVE Complete agreement or harmony.

   a. Ambiguous
   b. Unanimous
   c. Adulate
   d. Incredulous

39. VERB Seize power from another usually by illegitimate means.

   a. Trajectory
   b. Trapeze
   c. Usurp
   d. Benevolence

40. ADJECTIVE Saleable or marketable.

    a. Veneer
    b. Vendible
    c. Venison
    d. Veritable

41. Choose the best definition of importune.

    a. To find an opportunity
    b. To ask all the time.
    c. Cannot find an opportunity
    d. None of the above

42. Choose the best definition of volatile.

    a. Not explosive
    b. Catches fire easily
    c. Does not catch fire
    d. Explosive

43. Choose the best definition of plaintive.

    a. Happy
    b. Mournful
    c. Faint
    d. Plain

44. Choose the best definition of nexus.

    a. A connection
    b. A telephone switch
    c. Part of a computer
    d. None of the above

45. Choose the best definition of conjoin.

    a. A connection
    b. To marry
    c. Weld together
    d. To join together

46. Choose the best definition of petrify.

    a. Turn into a fossil
    b. Turn to stone
    c. Turn into wood
    d. Turn into glass

47. Choose the best definition of inherent.

    a. To receive money in a will
    b. An essential part of
    c. To receive money from a will
    d. None of the above

48. Choose the best definition of torpid.

    a. Fast
    b. Rapid
    c. Sluggish
    d. Violent

49. Choose the best definition of gregarious.

    a. Sociable
    b. Introverted
    c. Large
    d. Solitary

50. Choose the best definition of alloy.

a. To mix with something superior
b. To mix
c. To mix with something inferior
d. To purify

51. Choose the best definition of mollify.

a. To anger
b. To modify
c. To irritate
d. To soothe

52. Choose the best definition of redundant.

a. Backup
b. Necessary repetition
c. Unnecessary repetition
d. No repetition

53. Choose the best definition of bicker.

a. Chat
b. Discuss
c. Argue
d. Debate

54. Choose the best definition of sombre.

a. Gothic
b. Black
c. Serious
d. Evil

55. Choose the best definition of maverick.

a. Rebel
b. Conformist
c. Unconventional
d. Conventional

56. Choose the best definition of tenuous.

a. Strong
b. Tense
c. Firm
d. Weak

57. Choose the best definition of pandemonium.

a. Chaos
b. Orderly
c. Quiet
d. Noisy

58. Choose the best definition of perpetual.

a. Continuous
b. Slowly
c. Over a very long time
d. Motion

59. Choose the best definition of denigrate.

a. Compliment
b. Belittle
c. Praise
d. Admire

60. Choose the best definition of mundane.

   a. Exciting
   b. Continuous
   c. Unforgiving
   d. Ordinary

61. Choose the best definition of bedlam.

   a. In bed
   b. Out of bed
   c. Confusion
   d. Noise

62. Choose the best definition of avert.

   a. To prevent
   b. To look at
   c. To avenge
   d. To facilitate

63. Choose the best definition of dissipate.

   a. Drip
   b. Scatter
   c. Appear
   d. Degenerate

64. Choose the best definition of vexed.

   a. Hexed
   b. Amused
   c. Tickled
   d. Irritated

65. Choose the best definition of gaunt.

   a. Tall
   b. Very thin
   c. Thin
   d. Straight

66. Choose the best definition of epitaph.

   a. Inscription on a tomb
   b. Inscription on a building
   c. Gravestone
   d. None of the above

67. Choose the best definition of oblivion.

   a. Infinity
   b. Far away
   c. Lacking awareness
   d. Blackness

68. Choose the best definition of abhor.

   a. To hate
   b. To give up
   c. To neglect
   d. To throw out

69. Choose the best definition of remuneration.

   a. Give away
   b. Donation
   c. Pay
   d. Fee

70. Choose the best definition of abrasive.

a. Nasty
b. Sharp
c. Prickly
d. Rough

71. Choose the best definition of engender.

a. To cause
b. To create
c. For both genders
d. None of the above

72. Choose the best definition of credible.

a. Not believable
b. Believable
c. Sensible
d. Not sensible

73. Choose the best definition of harbinger.

a. Indicator
b. Puzzle
c. Warning
d. Danger

74. Choose the best definition of enigma.

a. Code
b. Puzzle
c. Secret
d. Password

75. Choose the best definition of tardy.

a. Late
b. Rude
c. Polite
d. Bitter

76. Choose the best definition of blatant.

a. Not clear
b. Obvious
c. Bland
d. Unusual taste

77. Choose the best definition of tawdry.

a. Cheap
b. Expensive
c. Drab
d. Thread bare

78. Choose the best definition of gullible.

a. Does not believe anything
b. Tells lies
c. Believes anything
d. None of the above

79. Choose the best definition of reprieve.

a. Postponement
b. Early start
c. Relief
d. None of the above

80. Choose the best definition of desist.

    a. Re-start

    b. Stop

    c. Start

    d. Stop for a moment

Answer Key

SECTION 1 – READING COMPREHENSION

1. A
Helen's parents hired Anne to teach Helen to communicate. Choice B is incorrect because the passage states Anne had trouble finding her way around, which means she could walk. Choice C is incorrect because you don't hire a teacher to teach someone to play. Choice D is incorrect because by age 6, if Helen had never eaten, she would have starved to death.

2. B
The correct answer because that fact is stated directly in the passage. The passage explains that Anne taught Helen to hear by allowing her to feel the vibrations in her throat.

3. A
We can infer that Anne is a patient teacher because she did not leave or lose her temper when Helen bit or hit her; she just kept trying to teach Helen. Choice B is incorrect because Anne taught Helen to read and talk. Choice C is incorrect because Anne could hear. She was partially blind, not deaf. Choice D is incorrect because it does not have to do with patience.

4. B
The passage states that it was hard for anyone but Anne to understand Helen when she spoke. Choice A is incorrect because the passage does not mention Helen spoke a foreign language. Choice C is incorrect because there is no mention of how quiet or loud Helen's voice was. Choice D is incorrect because we know from reading the passage that Helen did learn to speak.

5. D
This question tests the reader's summarization skills. The question is asking very generally about the message of the passage, and the title, "Ways Characters Communicate in Theater," is one indication of that. The other choices A, B, and C are all directly from the text, and therefore readers may be inclined to select one of them, but are too specific to encapsulate the entirety of the passage and its message.

6. B
The paragraph on soliloquies mentions "To be or not to be," and it is from the context of that paragraph that readers may understand that because "To be or not to be" is a soliloquy, Hamlet will be introspective, or thoughtful, while delivering it. It is true that actors deliver soliloquies alone, and may be "solitary" (choice A), but "thoughtful" (choice B) is more true to the overall idea of the paragraph. Readers may choose C because drama and theater can be used interchangeably and the passage mentions that soliloquies are unique to theater (and therefore drama), but this answer is not specific enough to the paragraph in question. Readers may pick up on the theme of life and death and Hamlet's true intentions and select that he is "hopeless" (choice D), but those themes are not discussed either by this paragraph or passage, as a close textual reading and analysis confirms.

7. C

This question tests the reader's grammatical skills. Choice B seems logical, but parenthesis are actually considered to be a stronger break in a sentence than commas are, and along this line of thinking, actually disrupt the sentence more.

Choices A and D make comparisons between theater and film that are not made in the passage, and may or may not be true. This detail does clarify the statement that asides are most unique to theater by adding that it is not completely unique to theater, which may have been why the author didn't chose not to delete it and instead used parentheses to designate the detail's importance (choice C).

8. A

Low blood sugar occurs both in diabetics and healthy adults.

9. B

None of the statements are the author's opinion.

10. A

The author's purpose is the inform.

11. A

The only statement that is not a detail is, "A doctor can diagnosis this medical condition by asking the patient questions and testing."

12. A

This sentence is a recommendation.

13. C

Tips for a good night's sleep is the best alternative title for this article.

14. B

Mental activity is helpful for a good night's sleep is can not be inferred from this article.

15. A

From the passage, one disadvantage of taking naps is they may keep you awake at night.

16. C

Based on the partial table of contents, you would find information about natural selection in the ecology section on page 110.

17. C

To be infamous means to be remembered for an evil or terrible action. Therefore, the word infamy means to remember a bad or terrible thing. Choice A is incorrect because being famous is not the same as being infamous. Choice B is incorrect because the attack on Pearl Harbor was not good. Choice D is incorrect because Pearl Harbor was not forgotten.

18. C
Each other answer set contains the name of at least one country that was not part of the AXIS powers.

19. D
It is stated in the passage. Choice A is not correct because there was no indication that Japan would attack San Diego
Choice B is incorrect because the attack on Pearl Harbor was a surprise. Choice C is incorrect because Roosevelt was not planning to attack Japan.

20. C
The passage clearly states that Japan planned a surprise attack. They chose that early time to catch the U.S. military off guard. Choice A is incorrect because the military does not sleep late. Choice B is incorrect because there is no law against bombing countries. Choice D is incorrect because it makes no sense.

21. C
This question tests the reader's vocabulary skills. The uses of the negatives "but" and "less," especially right next to each other, may confuse readers into answering with choices A or D, which list words that are antonyms to "militant." Readers may also be confused by the comparison of healthy people with what is being described as an overly healthy person--both people are good, but the reader may look for which one is "worse" in the comparison, and therefore stray toward the antonym words. One key to understanding the meaning of "militant" if the reader is unfamiliar with it is to look at the root of the word; readers can then easily associate it with "military" and gain a sense of what the word signifies: defence (especially considered that the immune system defends the body). Choice C is correct over choice B because "militant" is an adjective, just as the words in choice C are, whereas the words in choice B are nouns.

22. C
This question tests the reader's understanding of function within writing. The other choices are details included surrounding the quoted text, and may therefore confuse the reader. Choice A somewhat contradicts what is said earlier in the paragraph, which is that tests and treatments are improving, and probably doctors are along with them, but the paragraph doesn't actually mention doctors, and the subject of the question is the medicine. Choice B may seem correct to readers who aren't careful to understand that, while the author does mention the large number of people affected, the author is touching on the realities of living with allergies, rather than the likelihood of curing all allergies. Similarly, while the author does mention the "balance" of the body, which is easily associated with "wholesome," the author is not really making an argument and especially is not making an extreme statement that allergy medicines should be outlawed. Again, because the article's tone is on living with allergies, choice C is an appropriate choice that fits with the title and content of the text.

23. B
This question tests the reader's inference skills. The text does not state who is doing the recommending, but the use of the "patients," as well as the general context of the passage, lends itself to the logical partner, "doctors," choice B. The author does mention the recommendation but doesn't present it as her own (i.e. "I recommend that"), so

choice A may be eliminated. It may seem plausible that people with allergies (choice D) may recommend medicines or products to other people with allergies, but the text does not necessarily support this interaction taking place. Choice C may be selected because the EpiPen is specifically mentioned, but the use of the phrase "such as" when it is introduced is not limiting enough to assume the recommendation is coming from its creators.

24. D
This question tests the reader's global understanding of the text. Choice D includes the main topics of the three body paragraphs, and isn't too focused on a specific aspect or quote from the text, as the other questions are, giving a skewed summary of what the author intended. The reader may be drawn to choice B because of the title of the passage and the use of words like "better," but the message of the passage is larger and more general than this.

25. B
Reading the document posted to the Human Resources website is optional.

26. B
The document is recommended changes and have not be implemented yet.

27. C
This question tests the reader's summarization skills. The use of the word "actually" in describing what kind of people poets are, as well as other moments like this, may lead readers to selecting choices B or D, but the author is more information than trying to persuade readers. The author gives no indication that she loves poetry (choice B) or that people, students specifically (D), should write poems. Choice A is incorrect because the style and content of this paragraph do not match those of a foreword; forewords usually focus on the history or ideas of a specific poem to introduce it more fully and help it stand out against other poems. The author here focuses on several poems and gives broad statements. Instead, she tells a kind of story about poems, giving three very broad time periods in which to discuss them, thereby giving a brief history of poetry, as choice C states.

28. A
This question tests the reader's summarization skills. Key words in the topic sentences of each of the paragraphs ("oldest," "Renaissance," "modern") should give the reader an idea that the author is moving chronologically. The opening and closing sentence-paragraphs are broad and talk generally. B seems reasonable, but epic poems are mentioned in two paragraphs, eliminating the idea that only new types of poems are used in each paragraph. Choice C is also easily eliminated because the author clearly mentions several different poets, groups of people, and poems. Choice D also seems reasonable, considering that the author does move from older forms of poetry to newer forms, but use of "so (that)" makes this statement false, for the author gives no indication that she is rushing (the paragraphs are about the same size) or that she prefers modern poetry.

29. D
This question tests the reader's attention to detail. The key word is "invented"-- it ties together the Mesopotamians, who invented the written word, and the fact that they, as

the inventors, also invented and used poetry. The other selections focus on other details mentioned in the passage, such as that the Renaissance's admiration of the Greeks (choice C) and that Beowulf is in Old English (choice A). Choice B may seem like an attractive answer because it is unlike the others and because the idea of heroes seems rooted in ancient and early civilizations.

30. B
This question tests the reader's vocabulary and contextualization skills. "Telling" is not an unusual word, but it may be used here in a way that is not familiar to readers, as an adjective rather than a verb in gerund form. Choice A may seem like the obvious answer to a reader looking for a verb to match the use they are familiar with. If the reader understands that the word is being used as an adjective and that choice A is a ploy, they may opt to select choice D, "wordy," but it does not make sense in context. Choice C can be easily eliminated, and doesn't have any connection to the paragraph or passage. "Significant" (choice B) makes sense contextually, especially relative to the phrase "give insight" used later in the sentence.

SECTION II - VOCABULARY

1. C
Edify VERB to instruct or improve morally or intellectually.

2. B
Egress NOUN an exit or way out.

3. A
Confidential ADJECTIVE kept secret within a certain circle of persons; not intended to be known publicly.

4. C
Felony NOUN serious criminal offence that is punishable by death or imprisonment above a year.

5. B
Foment VERB to encourage or incite troublesome acts.

6. A
Funereal ADJECTIVE dignified, solemn that is appropriate for a funeral.

7. B
Geniality NOUN warmth and kindness of disposition.

8. C
Genteel ADJECTIVE polite and well mannered.

9. D
Goad VERB to encourage, stimulate or incite and provoke.

10. B

Heinous ADJECTIVE shocking, terrible or wicked.

11. A

Harbinger NOUN a person of thing that tells or announces the coming of someone or something.

12. D

Homologous ADJECTIVE similar or identical.

13. B

Ignoble ADJECTIVE common, not honorable or noble.

14. A

Immaterial ADJECTIVE irrelevant not having substance or matter.

15. A

Impeccable ADJECTIVE perfect, no faults or errors.

16. D

Juxtapose VERB place side by side for contrast or comparison.

17. D

Junta NOUN ruling council of a military government.

18. C

Laggard NOUN someone who takes more time than necessary.

19. B

Languid ADJECTIVE lacking enthusiasm, strength or energy.

20. D

Magnate NOUN a person of influence, rank or distinction.

21. C

Malady NOUN a lingering disease or ailment of the human body.

22. B

Nimble ADJECTIVE quick and light in movement.

23. B

Racket NOUN a loud noise.

24. C

Nuptial NOUN of or pertaining to wedding and marriage.

25. A

Ostensible ADJECTIVE meant for open display; apparent.

26. C
Octavo NOUN a sheet of paper 7 to 10 inches high and 4.5 to 6 inches wide, the size varying with the large original sheet used to create it. Made by folding the original sheet three times to produce eight leaves.

27. A
Pallid ADJECTIVE appearing weak, pale, or wan.

28. C
Panorama NOUN a picture or series of pictures representing a continuous scene.

29. B
Paradox NOUN a self contradictory statement that can only be true if false and vice versa.

30. A
Querulous ADJECTIVE often complaining; suggesting a complaint in expression; fretful, whining.

31. C
Quietus NOUN a stillness or pause; something that quiets or represses; removal from activity; especially: death.

32. B
Query NOUN question or inquiry.

33. B
Ravine NOUN a deep narrow valley or gorge in the earth's surface worn by running water.

34. C
Recede VERB move back or move away.

35. B
Shrivel VERB to become wrinkled.

36. C
Tannery NOUN a place where people tan hides to make leather.

37. B
Anecdote ADJECTIVE a brief amusing story.

38. B
Unanimous ADJECTIVE complete agreement or harmony.

39. C
Usurp VERB seize power from another usually from illegitimate means.

40. B
Vendible ADJECTIVE saleable or marketable.

41. B
Importune VERB to harass with persistent requests.

42. D
Volatile ADJECTIVE explosive.

43. B
Plaintive ADJECTIVE sorrowful, mournful or melancholic.

44. A
Nexus NOUN a form of connection.

45. D
Conjoin VERB to join together; to unite; to combine.

46. B
Petrify VERB to harden organic matter by permeating with water and depositing dissolved minerals.

47. B
Inherent ADJECTIVE naturally a part or consequence of something.

48. C
Torpid ADJECTIVE lazy, lethargic or apathetic.

49. A
Gregarious ADJECTIVE Describing one who enjoys being in crowds and socializing.

50. C
Alloy VERB to mix or combine; often used of metals.

51. D
Mollify VERB to ease a burden; make less painful; to comfort; soothe.

52. C
Redundant ADJECTIVE repetitive or needlessly wordy.

53. C
Bicker VERB to quarrel in a tiresome, insulting manner.

54. C
Sombre ADJECTIVE dark; gloomy.

55. A
Maverick NOUN showing independence in thoughts or actions.

56. D
Tenuous ADJECTIVE thin in substance or consistency.

57. A
Pandemonium NOUN chaos; tumultuous or lawless violence.

58. A
Perpetual ADJECTIVE continuing uninterrupted.

59. B
Denigrate VERB to treat as worthless; belittle, degrade or disparage.

60. D
Mundane ADJECTIVE ordinary; not new.

61. C
Bedlam NOUN a place or situation of chaotic uproar, and where confusion prevails.

62. A
Avert VERB to ward off, or prevent, the occurrence or effects of.

63. B
Dissipate VERB to drive away; scatter.

64. D
Vexed VERB annoyed, irritated or distressed.

65. B
Gaunt ADJECTIVE lean, angular and bony.

66. A
Epitaph NOUN an inscription on a gravestone in memory of the deceased.

67. C
Oblivion NOUN the state of forgetfulness or distraction.

68. A
Abhor VERB to regard with horror or detestation.

69. C
Remuneration NOUN a payment for work done; wages, salary, emolument.

70. D
Abrasive ADJECTIVE being rough and coarse in manner or disposition.

71. B
Engender VERB to give existence to; to produce.

72. B
Credible ADJECTIVE believable or plausible.

73. A
Harbinger NOUN a person or thing that foreshadows or foretells the coming of someone or something.

74. B
Enigma NOUN something puzzling, mysterious or inexplicable.

75. A
Tardy NOUN late, overdue or delayed.

76. B
Blatant ADJECTIVE Obvious; on show.

77. A
Tawdry ADJECTIVE cheap and gaudy; showy.

78. C
Gullible ADJECTIVE easily deceived or duped; naïve, easily cheated or fooled.

79. A
Reprieve ADJECTIVE The cancellation or postponement of a punishment.

80. B
Desist VERB to cease to proceed or act; to stop; to forbear. [4]

Practice Test Questions Set 2

Section I – Reading Comprehension

Questions: 30

Section II – Vocabulary

Questions: 80

This set of practice test questions presents questions that represent the type of question you should expect to find on the Nelson Denny. However, they are not intended to match exactly what is on the NDRT.

For the best results, take these practice questions as if it were the real exam. Set aside time when you will not be disturbed, and a location that is quiet and free of distractions. Read the instructions carefully, read each question carefully, and answer to the best of your ability.

Use the bubble answer sheets provided. When you have completed the practice questions, check your answer against the Answer Key and read the explanation provided.

Reading Comprehension Answer Sheet

1. A B C D   11. A B C D   21. A B C D
2. A B C D   12. A B C D   22. A B C D
3. A B C D   13. A B C D   23. A B C D
4. A B C D   14. A B C D   24. A B C D
5. A B C D   15. A B C D   25. A B C D
6. A B C D   16. A B C D   26. A B C D
7. A B C D   17. A B C D   27. A B C D
8. A B C D   18. A B C D   28. A B C D
9. A B C D   19. A B C D   29. A B C D
10. A B C D   20. A B C D   30. A B C D

Vocabulary Answer Sheet

1. A B C D
2. A B C D
3. A B C D
4. A B C D
5. A B C D
6. A B C D
7. A B C D
8. A B C D
9. A B C D
10. A B C D
11. A B C D
12. A B C D
13. A B C D
14. A B C D
15. A B C D
16. A B C D
17. A B C D
18. A B C D
19. A B C D
20. A B C D
21. A B C D
22. A B C D
23. A B C D
24. A B C D
25. A B C D
26. A B C D
27. A B C D
28. A B C D
29. A B C D
30. A B C D
31. A B C D
32. A B C D
33. A B C D
34. A B C D
35. A B C D
36. A B C D
37. A B C D
38. A B C D
39. A B C D
40. A B C D
41. A B C D
42. A B C D
43. A B C D
44. A B C D
45. A B C D
46. A B C D
47. A B C D
48. A B C D
49. A B C D
50. A B C D
51. A B C D
52. A B C D
53. A B C D
54. A B C D
55. A B C D
56. A B C D
57. A B C D
58. A B C D
59. A B C D
60. A B C D
61. A B C D
62. A B C D
63. A B C D
64. A B C D
65. A B C D
66. A B C D
67. A B C D
68. A B C D
69. A B C D
70. A B C D
71. A B C D
72. A B C D
73. A B C D
74. A B C D
75. A B C D
76. A B C D
77. A B C D
78. A B C D
79. A B C D
80. A B C D

Section I – Reading Comprehension.

Questions 1 - 4 refer to the following passage.

Passage 1 - The Crusades

In 1095 Pope Urban II proclaimed the First Crusade with the intent and stated goal to restore Christian access to holy places in and around Jerusalem. Over the next 200 years there were 6 major crusades and numerous minor crusades in the fight for control of the "Holy Land." Historians are divided on the real purpose of the Crusades, some believing that it was part of a purely defensive war against Islamic conquest; some see them as part of a long-running conflict at the frontiers of Europe; and others see them as confident, aggressive, papal-led expansion attempts by Western Christendom. The impact of the crusades was profound, and judgment of the Crusaders ranges from laudatory to highly critical. However, all agree that the Crusades and wars waged during those crusades were brutal and often bloody. Several hundred thousand Roman Catholic Christians joined the Crusades, they were Christians from all over Europe.

Europe at the time was under the Feudal System, so, while the Crusaders made vows to the Church, they also were beholden to their Feudal Lords. This led to the Crusaders not only fighting the Saracen, the commonly used word for Muslim at the time, but also each other for power and economic gain in the Holy Land. This infighting between the Crusaders is why many historians hold the view that the Crusades were simply a front for Europe to invade the Holy Land for economic gain in the name of the Church. Another factor contributing to this theory is that while the army of crusaders marched towards Jerusalem they pillaged the land as they went. The church and feudal Lords vowing to return the land to its original beauty, and inhabitants, this rarely happened though, as the Lords often kept the land for themselves. A full 800 years after the Crusades, Pope John Paul II expressed his sorrow for the massacre of innocent people and the lasting damage that the Medieval church caused.

1. What is the tone of this article?

    a. Subjective

    b. Objective

    c. Persuasive

    d. None of the Above

2. What can all historians agree on concerning the Crusades?

    a. It achieved great things

    b. It stabilized the Holy Land

    c. It was bloody and brutal

    d. It helped defend Europe from the Byzantine Empire

3. What impact did the feudal system have on the Crusades

   a. It unified the Crusaders

   b. It helped gather volunteers

   c. It had no effect on the Crusades

   d. It led to infighting, causing more damage than good

4. What does Saracen mean?

   a. Muslim

   b. Christian

   c. Knight

   d. Holy Land

Questions 5-8 refer to the following passage.

ABC Electric Warranty

ABC Electric Company warrants that its products are free from defects in material and workmanship. Subject to the conditions and limitations set forth below, ABC Electric will, at its option, either repair or replace any part of its products that prove defective due to improper workmanship or materials.

This limited warranty does not cover any damage to the product from improper installation, accident, abuse, misuse, natural disaster, insufficient or excessive electrical supply, abnormal mechanical or environmental conditions, or any unauthorized disassembly, repair, or modification.

This limited warranty also does not apply to any product on which the original identification information has been altered, or removed, has not been handled or packaged correctly, or has been sold as second-hand.

This limited warranty covers only repair, replacement, refund or credit for defective ABC Electric products, as provided above.

5. I tried to repair my ABC Electric blender, but could not, so can I get it repaired under this warranty?

   a. Yes, the warranty still covers the blender

   b. No, the warranty does not cover the blender

   c. Uncertain. ABC Electric may or may not cover repairs under this warranty

6. My ABC Electric fan is not working. Will ABC Electric provide a new one or repair this one?

   a. ABC Electric will repair my fan

   b. ABC Electric will replace my fan

   c. ABC Electric could either replace or repair my fan can request either a replacement or a repair.

7. My stove was damaged in a flood. Does this warranty cover my stove?

   a. Yes, it is covered.

   b. No, it is not covered.

   c. It may or may not be covered.

   d. ABC Electric will decide if it is covered

8. Which of the following is an example of improper workmanship?

   a. Missing parts

   b. Defective parts

   c. Scratches on the front

   d. None of the above

Questions 9 – 12 refer to the following passage.

Passage 2 - Women and Advertising

Only in the last few generations have media messages been so widespread and so readily seen, heard, and read by so many people. Advertising is an important part of both selling and buying anything from soap to cereal to jeans. For whatever reason, more consumers are women than are men. Media message are subtle but powerful, and more attention has been paid lately to how these message affect women.

Of all the products that women buy, makeup, clothes, and other stylistic or cosmetic products are among the most popular. This means that companies focus their advertising on women, promising them that their product will make her feel, look, or smell better than the next company's product will. This competition has resulted in advertising that is more and more ideal and less and less possible for everyday women. However, because women do look to these ideals and the products they represent as how they can potentially become, many women have developed unhealthy attitudes about themselves when they have failed to become those ideals.

In recent years, more companies have tried to change advertisements to be healthier for women. This includes featuring models of more sizes and addressing a huge outcry against unfair tools such as airbrushing and photo editing. There is debate about what the right balance between real and ideal is, because fashion is also considered art and some changes are made to elevate fashionable products purposefully and signify that they are creative, innovative, and the work of individual people. Artists want their freedom protected as much as women do, and advertising agencies are often caught in the middle.

Some claim that the companies who make these changes are not doing enough. Many people worry that there are still not enough models of different sizes and different ethnicities. Some people claim that companies use this healthier type of advertisement not for the good of women, but because they would like to sell products to the women who are looking for these kinds of messages. This is also a hard balance to find: companies need to make money, and women need to feel respected.

While the focus of this change has been on women, advertising can also affect men, and this change will hopefully be a lesson on media for all consumers.

9. The second paragraph states that advertising focuses on women

    a. to shape what the ideal should be

    b. because women buy makeup

    c. because women are easily persuaded

    d. because of the types of products that women buy

10. According to the passage, fashion artists and female consumers are at odds because

    a. there is a debate going on and disagreement drives people apart

    b. both of them are trying to protect their freedom to do something

    c. artists want to elevate their products above the reach of women

    d. women are creative, innovative, individual people

11. The author uses the phrase "for whatever reason" in this passage to

    a. keep the focus of the paragraph on media messages and not on the differences between men and women

    b. show that the reason for this is unimportant

    c. argue that it is stupid that more women are consumers than men

    d. show that he or she is tired of talking about why media messages are important

12. This passage suggests that

    a. advertising companies are still working on making their messages better

    b. all advertising companies seek to be more approachable for women

    c. women are only buying from companies that respect them

    d. artists could stop producing fashionable products if they feel bullied

Questions 13 - 16 refer to the following passage.

FDR, the Treaty of Versailles, and the Fourteen Points

At the conclusion of World War I, those who had won the war and those who were forced to admit defeat welcomed the end of the war and expected that a peace treaty would be signed. The American president, Franklin D. Roosevelt, played an important part in proposing what the agreements should be and did so through his Fourteen Points.
World War I had begun in 1914 when an Austrian archduke was assassinated, leading to a domino effect that pulled the world's most powerful countries into war on a large scale. The war catalyzed the creation and use of deadly weapons that had not previously existed, resulting in a great loss of soldiers on both sides of the fighting. More than 9 million soldiers were killed.

The United States agreed to enter the war right before it ended, and many believed that its decision to become finally involved brought on the end of the war. FDR made it very clear that the U.S. was entering the war for moral reasons and had an agenda focused on world peace. The Fourteen Points were individual goals and ideas (focused on peace, free trade, open communication, and self-reliance) that FDR wanted the power nations to strive for now that the war had ended. He was optimistic and had many ideas about what could be accomplished through, and during the post-war peace. However, FDR's fourteen points were poorly received when he presented them to the leaders of other world powers, many of whom wanted only to help their own countries and to punish the Germans for fueling the war, and they fell by the wayside. World War II was imminent, for Germany lost everything.

Some historians believe that the other leaders who participated in the Treaty of Versailles weren't receptive to the Fourteen Points because World War I was fought almost entirely on European soil, and the United States lost much less than did the other powers. FDR was in a unique position to determine the fate of the war, but doing it on his own terms did not help accomplish his goals. This is only one historical example of how the United State has tried to use its power as an important country, but found itself limited because of geological or ideological factors.

13. The main idea of this passage is that

    a. World War I was unfair because no fighting took place in America

    b. World War II happened because of the Treaty of Versailles

    c. the power the United States has to help other countries also prevents it from helping other countries

    d. Franklin D. Roosevelt was one of the United States' smartest presidents

14. According to the second paragraph, World War I started because

   a. an archduke was assassinated

   b. weapons that were more deadly had been developed

   c. a domino effect of allies agreeing to help one another

   d. the world's most powerful countries were large

15. The author includes the detail that 9 million soldiers were killed

   a. to demonstrate why European leaders were hesitant to accept peace

   b. to show the reader the dangers of deadly weapons

   c. to make the reader think about which countries lost the most soldiers

   d. to demonstrate why World War II was imminent

16. According to this passage, catalyzed means

   a. analyzed

   b. sped up

   c. invented

   d. funded

Questions 17 - 20 refer to the following passage.

Chocolate Chip Cookies

3/4 cup sugar
3/4 cup packed brown sugar
1 cup butter, softened
2 large eggs, beaten
1 teaspoon vanilla extract
2 1/4 cups all-purpose flour
1 teaspoon baking soda
3/4 teaspoon salt
2 cups semisweet chocolate chips
If desired, 1 cup chopped pecans, or chopped walnuts.
Preheat oven to 375 degrees.

Mix sugar, brown sugar, butter, vanilla and eggs in a large bowl. Stir in flour, baking soda, and salt. The dough will be very stiff.

Stir in chocolate chips by hand with a sturdy wooden spoon. Add the pecans, or other nuts, if desired. Stir until the chocolate chips and nuts are evenly dispersed.

Drop dough by rounded tablespoonfuls 2 inches apart onto a cookie sheet.

Bake 8 to 10 minutes, or, until light brown. Cookies may look underdone, but they will finish cooking after you take them out of the oven.

17. What is the correct order for adding these ingredients?

    a. Brown sugar, baking soda, chocolate chips

    b. Baking soda, brown sugar, chocolate chips

    c. Chocolate chips, baking soda, brown sugar

    d. Baking soda, chocolate chips, brown sugar

18. What does sturdy mean?

    a. Long

    b. Strong

    c. Short

    d. Wide

19. What does disperse mean?

    a. Scatter

    b. To form a ball

    c. To stir

    d. To beat

20. When can you stop stirring the nuts?

    a. When the cookies are cooked.

    b. When the nuts are evenly distributed.

    c. When the nuts are added.

    d. After the chocolate chips are added.

Questions 21 - 23 refer to the following passage.

Lowest Price Guarantee

Get it for less. Guaranteed!

ABC Electric will beat any advertised price by 10% of the difference.

    1) If you find a lower advertised price, we will beat it by 10% of the difference.

    2) If you find a lower advertised price within 30 days* of your purchase we will beat it by 10% of the difference.

3) If our own price is reduced within 30 days* of your purchase, bring in your receipt and we will refund the difference.

*14 days for computers, monitors, printers, laptops, tablets, cellular & wireless devices, home security products, projectors, camcorders, digital cameras, radar detectors, portable DVD players, DJ and pro-audio equipment, and air conditioners.

21. I bought a radar detector 15 days ago and saw an ad for the same model only cheaper. Can I get 10% of the difference refunded?

    a. Yes. Since it is less than 30 days, you can get 10% of the difference refunded.

    b. No. Since it is more than 14 days, you cannot get 10% of the difference refunded.

    c. It depends on the cashier.

    d. Yes. You can get the difference refunded.

22. I bought a flat-screen TV for $500 10 days ago and found an advertisement for the same TV, at another store, on sale for $400. How much will ABC refund under this guarantee?

    a. $100

    b. $110

    c. $10

    d. $400

23. What is the purpose of this passage?

    a. To inform

    b. To educate

    c. To persuade

    d. To entertain

Questions 24 - 27 refer to the following passage.

Passage 6 - What Is Mardi Gras?

Mardi Gras is fast becoming one of the South's most famous and most celebrated holidays. The word Mardi Gras comes from the French and the literal translation is "Fat Tuesday." The holiday has also been called Shrove Tuesday, due to its associations with Lent. The purpose of Mardi Gras is to celebrate and enjoy before the Lenten season of fasting and repentance begins.

What originated by the French Explorers in New Orleans, Louisiana in the 17th century is now celebrated all over the world. Panama, Italy, Belgium and Brazil all host large scale Mardi Gras celebrations, and many smaller cities and towns celebrate this fun loving Tuesday as well. Usually held in February or early March, Mardi Gras is a day of extravagance, a day for people to eat, drink and be merry, to wear costumes, masks and to dance to jazz music.

The French explorers on the Mississippi River would be in shock today if they saw the opulence of the parades and floats that grace the New Orleans streets during Mardi Gras these days. Parades in New Orleans are divided by organizations. These are more commonly known as Krewes.

Being a member of a Krewe is quite a task because Krewes are responsible for overseeing the parades. Each Krewe's parade is ruled by a Mardi Gras "King and Queen." The role of the King and Queen is to "bestow" gifts on their adoring fans as the floats ride along the street. They throw doubloons, which is fake money and usually colored green, purple and gold, which are the colors of Mardi Gras. Beads in those color shades are also thrown and cups are thrown as well. Beads are by far the most popular souvenir of any Mardi Gras parade, with each spectator attempting to gather as many as possible.

24. The purpose of Mardi Gras is to

   a. Repent for a month.

   b. Celebrate in extravagant ways.

   c. Be a member of a Krewe.

   d. Explore the Mississippi.

25. From reading the passage we can infer that "Kings and Queens"

   a. Have to be members of a Krewe.

   b. Have to be French.

   c. Have to know how to speak French.

   d. Have to give away their own money.

26. Which group of people began to hold Mardi Gras celebrations?

   a. Settlers from Italy

   b. Members of Krewes

   c. French explorers

   d. Belgium explorers

27. In the context of the passage, what does the word spectator mean?

    a. Someone who participates actively

    b. Someone who watches the parade's action

    c. Someone on the parade floats

    d. Someone who does not celebrate Mardi Gras

Questions 28 - 30 refer to the following passage.

Passage 7 - Firefighters

Firefighters are rescuers trained to put out any type of fire. There are fire departments in almost every country in the world, and they are one of the three main emergency services, along with the police department and the emergency medical services.

Firefighters receive extensive training in fire fighting to assure that they are prepared to handle any situation. While on duty, firemen or firewomen might have to deal with fire prevention, fire suppression, ventilation, containment, search and rescue, and many others.

The main goal of the fire departments is to save lives, protect property, and protect the environment from the dangers of a big fire. Traditionally, the firefighters are associated with Dalmatians as helper animals. While most fire departments use dogs, they are not Dalmatians. Fire departments only use dogs for rescue operations, and keep them away from fires.

28. What are the three main emergency services?

    a. fire departments, emergency medical and police

    b. fire departments, emergency medical and highway patrol

    c. RCMP, fire departments and emergency medical

    d. Disaster relief, fire departments, and emergency medical

29. What are the main goals of the fire department?

    a. put out fires and protect property

    b. to save lives, protect property and protect the environment

    c. to save lives, put out fires and protect property

    d. to protect property, save the environment and put out fires

30. What animal is traditionally associated with firefighters?

   a. Dogs
   b. Dalmatians
   c. Horses
   d. No animals are associated with firefighters

SECTION II - VOCABULARY

Choose the best word for the given definition.

1. NOUN Use of too many words.

   a. Verbiage
   b. Outspoken
   c. Inveigh
   d. Precarious

2. NOUN An aide or assistant.

   a. Attache
   b. Influx
   c. Mien
   d. Knoll

3. VERB To cause or inflict especially related to harm or injury.

   a. Wreak
   b. Mandible
   c. Tremulous
   d. Juxtapose

Practice Test Questions Set 2

4. ADJECTIVE Foolish, without understanding.

a. Coinage
b. Witless
c. Distinctive
d. Nullify

5. ADJECTIVE Strong fear of strangers.

a. Xenophobia
b. Agoraphobia
c. Frightful
d. Genteel

6. NOUN Highest point, highest state, or peak,.

a. Towering
b. Flickers
c. Zenith
d. Grouse

7. NOUN Light wind or gentle breeze.

a. Sea-breeze
b. Scuttle
c. Zephyr
d. Freight

8. NOUN Self-evident or clear obvious truth.

a. Truism
b. Catharsis
c. Libertine
d. Tractable

9. ADJECTIVE Beyond what is obvious or evident.

a. Ulterior
b. Sybarite
c. Torsion
d. Trenchant

10. ADJECTIVE Tasteless or bland.

a. Obstinate
b. Morose
c. Inculpate
d. Vapid

11. NOUN homeless child or stray.

a. Elegy
b. Waif
c. Martyr
d. Palaver

12. VERB Complaint or criticism.

a. Obsequies
b. Whine
c. Opprobrious
d. Panacea

13. NOUN Subordinate of lesser rank or authority.

a. Palliate
b. Plebeian
c. Underling
d. Expiate

14. NOUN A young animal that is between 1 and 2 years.

    a. Yearling
    b. Rogue
    c. Gnostic
    d. Billet

15. NOUN Lush green vegetation.

    a. Coquette
    b. Verdure
    c. Ennui
    d. Lugubrious

16. NOUN A person who is very passionate and fanatic about his specific objectives or beliefs.

    a. Plebeian
    b. Zealot
    c. Progenitor
    d. Iconoclast

17. NOUN Dizziness.

    a. Indolence
    b. Percipient
    c. Vertigo
    d. Tenacious

18. ADJECTIVE Obvious or easy to notice.

    a. Important
    b. Conspicuous
    c. Beautiful
    d. Convincing

19. NOUN Disposition to do good.

    a. Happiness
    b. Courage
    c. Kindness
    d. Benevolence

20. ADJECTIVE Full of energy; exuberant; noisy.

    a. Boisterous
    b. Soft
    c. Gentle
    d. Warm

21. VERB To fondle.

    a. Hold
    b. Caress
    c. Facilitate
    d. Neuter

22. ADJECTIVE Outstanding in importance.

    a. Momentous
    b. Spurious
    c. Extraordinary
    d. Secede

23. NOUN An opponent or enemy.

    a. Antagonist
    b. Protagonist
    c. Sophist
    d. Pugilist

Practice Test Questions Set 2

24. NOUN A keepsake; an object kept as a reminder of a place or event.

  a. Monument
  b. Memento
  c. Recurrence
  d. Catharsis

25. ADJECTIVE Producing harm in a stealthy, often gradual, manner.

  a. Adulterate
  b. Acquiesce
  c. Insidious
  d. Deceitful

26. NOUN A route or proposed route of a journey.

  a. Schedule
  b. Guidebook
  c. Itinerary
  d. Diary

27. ADJECTIVE Dignified.

  a. Rich
  b. Noble
  c. Gallant
  d. Illustrious

28. ADJECTIVE Sharp deep cutting or biting.

  a. Trenchant
  b. Apprehensible
  c. Bulbous
  d. Invidious

29. VERB To kiss or related to kissing.

  a. Knead
  b. Defalcate
  c. Upbraid
  d. Osculate

30. NOUN Change or alteration.

  a. Mutation
  b. Veracity
  c. Oration
  d. Facet

31. ADJECTIVE Flexible or plaint.

  a. Facile
  b. Lithe
  c. Misanthropic
  d. Prescient

32. VERB To express displeasure or indignation.

  a. Sanction
  b. Resent
  c. Venerate
  d. Cull

33. ADJECTIVE Fat, plump and overweight.

  a. Chubby
  b. Corrigible
  c. Heathenish
  d. Peccant

34. ADJECTIVE Fearful or timid.

   a. Skittish
   b. Pervious
   c. Prefatory
   d. Reparable

35. ADJECTIVE Harsh or rough sounding.

   a. Rambunctious
   b. Unctuous
   c. Exorbitant
   d. Cardinal

36. ADJECTIVE Indicating or expressing a cause.

   a. Averse
   b. Nominal
   c. Reprehensible
   d. Causal

37. ADJECTIVE Able to be kept under restraint or control.

   a. Rampant
   b. Repressible
   c. Exigent
   d. Exemplary

38. ADJECTIVE Living both on land and in water.

   a. Amicable
   b. Fervid
   c. Amphibious
   d. Frigid

39. VERB To imbue with life or animation.

   a. Grapple
   b. Galvanize
   c. Luxuriate
   d. Mete

40. NOUN A slight degree of difference in anything perceptible to the sense of the mind.

   a. Nuance
   b. Omission
   c. Peerage
   d. Petulance

41. Choose the best definition of obfuscate.

   a. Deliberately make noisy
   b. Deliberately make difficult
   c. Deliberately make quiet
   d. Talk about for a long time

42. Choose the best definition of plethora.

   a. Too many
   b. Too few
   c. A lot
   d. A few

43. Choose the best definition of laceration.

   a. A stripe
   b. A mark
   c. A scratch
   d. A cut

44. Choose the best definition of enshroud.

a. Hold up
b. Cover
c. Wear
d. Take away

45. Choose the best definition of hasten.

a. To hurry
b. To climb
c. To fasten
d. To worry

46. Choose the best definition of pliable.

a. Rigid
b. Fixable
c. Bend able
d. None of the Above

47. Choose the best definition of blithe.

a. Skinny
b. Tall
c. Carefree
d. Lithe

48. Choose the best definition of rescind.

a. To take back
b. To give away
c. To enforce
d. To straighten

49. Choose the best definition of headstrong.

a. Does not listen
b. Stubborn
c. Willing
d. To disbelieve

50. Choose the best definition of oblique.

a. Direct
b. Indirect
c. Sharp
d. Straight

51. Choose the best definition of temper.

a. To make worse
b. To aggravate
c. To soften
d. None of the Above

52. Choose the best definition of cryptic.

a. Building in a graveyard
b. Difficult to understand
c. Printed in code
d. None of the above

53. Choose the best definition of curtail.

a. To cut short
b. To arrive early
c. To lengthen
d. To give back

54. Choose the best definition of heed.

a. To ignore
b. To listen
c. To advise
d. To pay

55. Choose the best definition of oblivious.

a. Far Away
b. Believable
c. Unbelievable
d. Totally unaware

56. Choose the best definition of podium.

a. Speaker
b. Raised platform
c. Brief lecture
d. None of the above

57. Choose the best definition of boorish.

a. Bad tempered
b. Bad mannered
c. Bad looking
d. Bad smelling

58. Choose the best definition of heresy.

a. Against the orthodox opinion
b. Same as the orthodox opinion
c. An unusual opinion
d. To have no opinion

59. Choose the best definition of respite.

a. A drink
b. Intermission
c. A rest stop on highways
d. An interval

60. Choose the best definition of regicide.

a. To endow or furnish with requisite ability
b. Killing a king
c. Disposed to seize by violence or by unlawful or greedy methods
d. To refresh after labor

61. Choose the best definition of salient.

a. To make light by fermentation, as dough
b. Not stringent or energetic
c. Negligible
d. Worthy of note or relevant

62. Choose the best definition of sedentary.

a. Yellowing of the skin
b. Not moving or sitting in one a place
c. To wander from place to place
d. Perplexity

Practice Test Questions Set 2

63. Choose the best definition of sedulous.

a. The support on or against which a lever rests

b. Dedicated and diligent

c. To oppose with an equal force

d. The branch of medical science that relates to improving health

64. Choose the best definition of tincture.

a. Alcoholic drink with plant extract used for medicine

b. An artificial trance-sleep

c. A special medicinal drink made by mixing water with plant extracts

d. The point of puncture

65. Choose the best definition of truism.

a. A comparison which directs the mind to the representative object itself

b. Self-evident or clear obvious truth

c. A statement that is true but that can hardly be proved

d. False statements

66. Choose the best definition of mutation.

a. To utter with a loud and vehement voice

b. Change or alteration

c. An act or exercise of will

d. To cause to be one

67. Choose the best definition of alchemy.

a. Small in size

b. Change metal into gold

c. Flexible or pliant

d. Fake

68. Choose the best definition of benchmark.

a. A standard of measure

b. To cause boredom

c. Clumsy

d. Strong feelings of love

69. Choose the best definition of pudgy.

a. To draw general inferences

b. Fat, plump and overweight

c. Permanence

d. Spoilt or bad condition

70. Choose the best definition of timorous.

a. Fearful or timid

b. Third from last

c. Reprove; accuse; condemn

d. Happy

71. Choose the best definition of raucous.

a. Pedantic; academic; for teaching

b. Contemptuous, scornful

c. Not essential under the circumstances

d. Harsh or rough sounding

72. Choose the best definition of abet.

a. To aid, help
b. To reject
c. To kidnap
d. To fly

73. Choose the best definition of adorn.

a. To decorate
b. To dismantle
c. To stick something to
d. To outline vaguely

74. Choose the best definition of allege.

a. To summarize
b. To re-distribute
c. To say without proof
d. To increase

75. Choose the best definition of nomadic.

a. Happening at night
b. Wandering
c. Unyielding
d. Foreboding

76. Choose the best definition of appease.

a. To take, or make use of
b. Shock or disgust
c. To take without justification
d. To calm or satisfy

77. Choose the best definition of opulent.

a. Ostentatiously rich and lavish
b. Appearing as such
c. Greatest in importance
d. Easily understood

78. Choose the best definition of perfunctory.

a. With little interest or enthusiasm
b. Flippant or bold
c. Difficult to understand
d. Skillful

79. Choose the best definition of flout.

a. To give up
b. To disregard or disobey
c. To absorb or engross
d. To make an impression

80. Choose the best definition of indefatigable.

a. Incapable of defeat
b. Not changeable
c. Assumed to be true
d. Talkative or wordy

Answer Key

SECTION I - READING COMPREHENSION

1. A
Choice B is incorrect; the author did not express their opinion on the subject matter. Choice C is incorrect, the author was not trying to prove a point.

2. C
Choice C is correct; historians believe it was brutal and bloody. Choice A is incorrect; there is no consensus that the Crusades achieved great things. Choice B is incorrect; it did not stabilize the Holy Lands. Choice D is incorrect, some historians do believe this was the purpose but not all historians.

3. D
The feudal system led to infighting. Choice A is incorrect, it had the opposite effect. Choice B is incorrect, though this is a good answer, it is not the best answer. The Church asked for volunteers not the Feudal Lords. Choice C is incorrect, it did have an effect on the Crusades.

4. A
Saracen was a generic term for Muslims widely used in Europe during the later medieval era.

5. B
This warranty does not cover a product that you have tried to fix yourself. From paragraph two, "This limited warranty does not cover ... any unauthorized disassembly, repair, or modification."

6. C
ABC Electric could either replace or repair the fan, provided the other conditions are met. ABC Electric has the option to repair or replace.

7. B
The warranty does not cover a stove damaged in a flood. From the passage, "This limited warranty does not cover any damage to the product from improper installation, accident, abuse, misuse, natural disaster, insufficient or excessive electrical supply, abnormal mechanical or environmental conditions."

A flood is an "abnormal environmental condition," and a natural disaster, so it is not covered.

8. A
A missing part is an example of defective workmanship. This is an error made in the manufacturing process. A defective part is not considered workmanship.

9. D
This question tests the reader's summarization skills. The other choices A, B, and C focus on portions of the second paragraph that are too narrow and do not relate to the

specific portion of text in question. The complexity of the sentence may mislead students into selecting one of these answers, but rearranging or restating the sentence will lead the reader to the correct answer. In addition, choice A makes an assumption that may or may not be true about the intentions of the company, choice B focuses on one product rather than the idea of the products, and choice C makes an assumption about women that may or may not be true and is not supported by the text.

10. B
This question tests reader's attention to detail. If a reader selects A, he or she may have picked up on the use of the word "debate" and assumed, very logically, that the two are at odds because they are fighting; however, this is simply not supported in the text. Choice C also uses very specific quotes from the text, but it rearranges and gives them false meaning. The artists want to elevate their creations above the creations of other artists, thereby showing that they are "creative" and "innovative." Similarly, choice D takes phrases straight from the text and rearranges and confuses them. The artists are described as wanting to be "creative, innovative, individual people," not the women.

11. A
This question tests reader's vocabulary and summarization skills. This phrase, used by the author, may seem flippant and dismissive if readers focus on the word "whatever" and misinterpret it as a popular, colloquial term. In this way, choices B and C may mislead the reader to selecting one of them by including the terms "unimportant" and "stupid," respectively. Choice D is a similar misreading, but doesn't make sense when the phrase is at the beginning of the passage and the entire passage is on media messages. Choice A is literally and contextually appropriate, and the reader can understand that the author would like to keep the introduction focused on the topic the passage is going to discuss.

12. A
This question tests a reader's inference skills. The extreme use of the word "all" in choice B suggests that every single advertising company are working to be approachable, and while this is not only unlikely, the text specifically states that "more" companies have done this, signifying that they have not all participated, even if it's a possibility that they may some day. The use of the limiting word "only" in choice C lends that answer similar problems; women are still buying from companies who do not care about this message, or those companies would not be in business, and the passage specifies that "many" women are worried about media messages, but not all. Readers may find choice D logical, especially if they are looking to make an inference, and while this may be a possibility, the passage does not suggest or discuss this happening. Choice A is correct based on specifically because of the relation between "still working" in the answer and "will hopefully" and the extensive discussion on companies struggles, which come only with progress, in the text.

13. C
This question tests the reader's summarization skills. The entire passage is leading up to the idea that the president of the US may not have had grounds to assert his Fourteen Points when other countries had lost so much. Choice A is pretty directly inferred by the text, but it does not adequately summarize what the entire passage is trying to communicate. Choice B may also be inferred by the passage when it says that the war is "imminent," but it does not represent the entire message, either. The passage does

seem to be in praise of FDR, or at least in respect of him, but it does not in any way claim that he is the smartest president, nor does this represent the many other points included. Choice C is then the obvious answer, and most directly relates to the closing sentences which it rewords.

14. C
This question tests the reader's attention to detail. The passage does state that choices A and B are true, and while those statements are in proximity to the explanation for why the war started, they are not the reason given. Choice D is a mix up of words used in the passage, which says that the largest powers were in play but not that this fact somehow started the war. The passage does make a direct statement that a domino effect started the war, supporting choice C as the correct answer.

15. A
This question tests the reader's understanding of functions in writing. Throughout the passage, it states that leaders of other nations were hesitant to accept generous or peaceful terms because of the grievances of the war, and the great loss of life was chief among these. While the passage does touch on the devastation of deadly weapons (B), the use of this raw, emotional fact serves a much larger purpose, and the focus of the passage is not the weapons. While readers may indeed consider who lost the most soldiers (C) when, so many countries were involved and the inequalities of loss are mentioned in the passage, there is no discussion of this in the passage. Choice D is related to A, but choice A is more direct and relates more to the passage.

16. B
This question tests the reader's vocabulary skills. Choice A may seem appealing to readers because it is phonetically similar to "catalyzed," but the two are not related in any other way. Choice C makes sense in context, but if plugged in to the sentence creates a redundancy that doesn't make sense. Choice D does also not make sense contextually, even if the reader may consider that funds were needed to create more weaponry, especially if it was advanced.

17. A
The correct order of ingredients is brown sugar, baking soda and chocolate chips.

18. B
Sturdy: strong, solid in structure or person. In context, Stir in chocolate chips by hand with a *sturdy* wooden spoon.

19. A
Disperse: to scatter in different directions or break up. In context, Stir until the chocolate chips and nuts are evenly *dispersed*.

20. B
You can stop stirring the nuts when they are evenly distributed. From the passage, "Stir until the chocolate chips and nuts are evenly dispersed."

21. B
The time limit for radar detectors is 14 days. Since you made the purchase 15 days ago, you do not qualify for the guarantee.

22. B
Since you made the purchase 10 days ago, you are covered by the guarantee. Since it is an advertised price at a different store, ABC Electric will "beat" the price by 10% of the difference, which is,

500 – 400 = 100 – difference in price

100 X 10% = $10 – 10% of the difference

The advertised lower price is $400. ABC will beat this price by 10% so they will refund $100 + 10 = $110.

23. C
The purpose of this passage is to persuade.

24. B
The correct answer can be found in the fourth sentence of the first paragraph.

Choice A is incorrect because repenting begins the day AFTER Mardi Gras. Choice C is incorrect because you can celebrate Mardi Gras without being a member of a Krewe.

Choice D is incorrect because exploration does not play any role in a modern Mardi Gras celebration.

25. A
The second sentence is the last paragraph states that Krewes are led by the Kings and Queens. Therefore, you must have to be part of a Krewe to be its King or its Queen.

Choice B is incorrect because it never states in the passage that only people from France can be Kings and Queen of Mardi Gras

Choice C is incorrect because the passage says nothing about having to speak French.

Choice D is incorrect because the passage does state that the Kings and Queens throw doubloons, which is fake money.

26. C
The first sentences of BOTH the 2nd and 3rd paragraphs mention that French explorers started this tradition in New Orleans.
Choices A, B and D are incorrect because they are names of cities or countries listed in the 2nd paragraph.

27. B
In the final paragraph, the word spectator is used to describe people who are watching the parade and catching cups, beads and doubloons.
Choices A and C are incorrect because we know the people who participate are part of Krewes. People who work the floats and parades are also part of Krewes

Choice D is incorrect because the passage makes no mention of people who do not celebrate Mardi Gras.

28. A
The three main emergency services are fire departments, emergency medical and police.

29. B
The three goals of the fire department are to save lives, protect property and protect the environment.

30. B
Dalmatians are traditionally associated with fire fighters.

SECTION II - VOCABULARY

1. A
Verbiage NOUN speech with too many words.

2. A
Attache NOUN an aide or assistant.

3. A
Wreak VERB to cause or inflict especially related to harm or injury.

4. B
Witless ADJECTIVE foolish, without understanding.

5. A
Xenophobia NOUN a strong fear of strangers.

6. C
Zenith NOUN highest point, highest state, or peak,.

7. C
Zephyr NOUN light wind or gentle breeze.

8. A
Truism NOUN self-evident or clear obvious truth.

9. A
Ulterior ADJECTIVE beyond what is obvious or evident.

10. D
Vapid ADJECTIVE tasteless or bland.

11. B
Waif NOUN homeless child or stray.

12. B
Whine VERB Complaint or criticism.

13. C
Underling NOUN subordinate of lesser rank or authority.

14. A
Yearling NOUN a young animal that is between 1 and 2 years.

15. B
Verdure NOUN lush green vegetation.

16. B
Zealot NOUN a person who is very passionate and fanatic about his specific objectives or beliefs.

17. C
Vertigo NOUN dizziness.

18. B
Conspicuous ADJECTIVE obvious or easy to notice.

19. D
Benevolence NOUN disposition to do good.

20. A
Boisterous ADJECTIVE full of energy; exuberant; noisy.

21. B
Fondle VERB to touch or stroke.

22. A
Momentous ADJECTIVE outstanding in importance.

23. A
Antagonist NOUN an opponent or enemy.

24. B
Memento NOUN a keepsake; an object kept as a reminder of a place or event.

25. C
Insidious ADJECTIVE producing harm in a stealthy, often gradual, manner.

26. C
Itinerary NOUN a route or proposed route of a journey.

27. D
Illustrious ADJECTIVE dignified.

28. A
Trenchant ADJECTIVE sharp deep cutting or biting.

29. D
Osculate VERB to kiss or related to kissing.

30. A
Mutation NOUN change or alteration.

31. B
Lithe ADJECTIVE flexible or plaint.

32. B
Resent VERB to express displeasure or indignation.

33. A
Chubby ADJECTIVE fat, plump and overweight.

34. A
Skittish ADJECTIVE fearful or timid.

35. A
Rambunctious ADJECTIVE harsh or rough sounding.

36. D
Causal ADJECTIVE indicating or expressing a cause.

37. B
Repressible ADJECTIVE able to be kept under restraint or control.

38. C
Amphibious ADJECTIVE living both on land and in water.

39. B
Galvanize VERB to imbue with life or animation.

40. A
Nuance NOUN a slight degree of difference in anything perceptible to the sense of the mind.

41. B
Obfuscate VERB to deliberately make more confusing to conceal the truth.

42. A
Plethora NOUN an excessive amount or number; an abundance.

43. D
Laceration NOUN an irregular open wound caused by a blunt impact to soft tissue.

44. B

Enshroud VERB to cover with (or as if with) a shroud.

45. A

Hasten VERB to move in a quick fashion.

46. C

Pliable ADJECTIVE soft, flexible, easily bent; formed, shaped or molded.

47. C

Carefree ADJECTIVE indifferent, careless, showing a lack of concern.

48. A

Rescind VERB to repeal, annul, or declare void; to take (something such as a rule or contract) out of effect.

49. B

Headstrong ADJECTIVE determined to do as one pleases, and not as others want.

50. B

Oblique ADJECTIVE not straightforward; indirect; obscure; hence, disingenuous; underhand; perverse; sinister.

51. C

Temper VERB to moderate or control.

52. B

Cryptic ADJECTIVE mystified or of an obscure nature.

53. A

Curtail VERB to shorten or abridge the duration of something; to truncate.

54. B

Heed VERB to mind; to regard with care; to take notice of; to attend to; to observe.

55. D

Oblivious ADJECTIVE lacking awareness; unmindful.

56. B

Podium NOUN a platform on which to stand, as when conducting an orchestra or preaching at a pulpit.

57. B

Boorish ADJECTIVE behaving as a boor; rough in manners; rude; uncultured.

58. A

Heresy NOUN a controversial or unorthodox opinion held by a member of a group, as in politics, philosophy or science.

59. B
Respite NOUN a brief interval of rest or relief.

60. B
Regicide VERB to kill a king.

61. D
Salient ADJECTIVE worthy of note or relevant.

62. B
Sedentary ADJECTIVE not moving or sitting in one place.

63. B
Sedulous ADJECTIVE dedicated and diligent.

64. A
Tincture NOUN alcoholic drink with plant extract used for medicine.

65. B
Truism NOUN self-evident or clear obvious truth.

66. B
Mutation NOUN change or alteration.

67. B
Alchemy NOUN medieval chemical philosophy aimed at trying to change metal into gold.

68. A
Benchmark NOUN a standard of measure.

69. B
Pudgy ADJECTIVE fat, plump and overweight.

70. A
Timorous ADJECTIVE fearful or timid.

71. D
Raucous ADJECTIVE harsh or rough sounding.

72. A
Abet VERB to aid, help.

73. A
Adorn VERB to decorate.

74. C
Allege VERB to say without proof.

75. B
Nomadic ADJECTIVE wandering.

76. D
Appease VERB to calm or satisfy.

77. A
Opulent ADJECTIVE ostentatiously rich and lavish.

78. A
Perfunctory ADJECTIVE with little interest or enthusiasm.

79. B
Flout VERB to disregard or disobey.

80. A
Indefatigable ADJECTIVE incapable of defeat.

Practice Tests 3 & 4

Join us online for over 150 more practice questions (completely FREE) including a timed Nelson Denny Test to get ready for the real thing!

Go to https://courses.test-preparation.ca/course/nelsondenny-police-3-4

and use coupon NDRT34

NOTE: there is not charge - you must register and use the coupon above.

How to Improve your Vocabulary

VOCABULARY TESTS CAN BE DAUNTING WHEN YOU THINK OF THE ENORMOUS NUMBER OF WORDS THAT MIGHT COME UP IN THE EXAM. As the exam date draws near, your anxiety will grow because you know that no matter how many words you memorize, chances are, you will still remember so few. Here are some tips which you can use to hurdle the big words that may come up in your exam without having to open the dictionary and memorize all the words known to humankind.

Build up and tear apart the big words. Big words, like many other things, are composed of small parts. Some words are made up of many other words. A man who lifts weights for example, is a weight lifter. Words are also made up of word parts called prefixes, suffixes and roots. Often times, we can see the relationship of different words through these parts. A person who is skilled with both hands is ambidextrous. A word with double meaning is ambiguous. A person with two conflicting emotions is ambivalent. Two words with synonymous meanings often have the same root. Bio, a root word derived from Latin is used in words like biography meaning to write about a person's life, and biology meaning the study of living organisms.

- **Words with double meanings.** Did you know that the word husband not only means a man married to a woman, but also thrift or frugality? Sometimes, words have double meanings. The dictionary meaning, or the denotation of a word is sometimes different from the way we use it or its connotation.

- **Read widely, read deeply and read daily.** The best way to expand your vocabulary is to familiarize yourself with as many words as possible through reading. By reading, you are able to remember words in a proper context and thus, remember its meaning or at the very least, its use. Reading widely would help you get acquainted with words you may never use every day. This is the best strategy without doubt. However, if you are studying for an exam next week, or even tomorrow, it isn't much help! Below you will find a range of different ways to learn new words quickly and efficiently.

- **Remember.** Always remember that big words are easy to understand when divided into smaller parts, and the smaller words will often have several other meanings aside from the one you already know.

Here are suggested effective ways to help you improve your vocabulary.

Be Committed To Learning New Words. To improve your vocabulary you need to make a commitment to learn new words. Commit to learning at least a word or two a day. You can also get new words by reading books, poems, stories, plays and magazines. Expose yourself to more language to increase the number of new words that you learn.

- **Learn Practical Vocabulary.** As much as possible, learn vocabulary that is associated with what you do and that you can use regularly. For example learn words related to your profession or hobby. Learn as much vocabulary as you can in your favorite subjects.

- **Use New Words Frequently.** When you learn a new word start using it and do so frequently. Repeat it when you are alone and try to use the word as often as you can with people you talk to. You can also use flashcards to practice new words that you learn.

- **Learn the Proper Usage.** If you do not understand the proper usage, look it up and make sure you have it right.

- **Use a Dictionary.** When reading textbooks, novels or assigned readings, keep the dictionary nearby. Also learn how to use online dictionaries and WORD dictionary. When you come across a new word, check for its meaning. If you cannot do so immediately, then you should write it down and check it when possible. This will help you understand what the word means and exactly how best to use it.

- **Learn Word Roots, Prefixes and Suffixes.** English words are usually derived from suffixes, prefixes and roots, which come from Latin, French or Greek. Learning the root or origin of a word helps you easily understand the meaning of the word and other words that are derived from the root. Generally, if you learn the meaning of one root word, you will understand two or three words. This is a great two-for-one strategy. Most prefixes, suffixes, roots and stems are used in two, three or more words, so if you know the root, prefix or suffix, you can guess the meaning of many words.

- **Synonyms and Antonyms.** Most words in the English language have two or three (at least) synonyms and antonyms. For example, "big," in the most common usage, has about seventy-five synonyms and an equal number of antonyms. Understanding the relationships between these words and how they all fit together gives your brain a framework, which makes them easier to learn, remember and recall.

- **Use Flash Cards.** Flash cards are one of the best ways to memorize things. They can be used anywhere and anytime, so you can use free moments waiting for the bus or waiting in line. Make your own or buy commercially prepared flash cards, and keep them with you all the time. See https://www.test-preparation.ca/flash-cards/

- **Make word lists.** Learning vocabulary, like learning many things, requires repetition. Keep a new words journal in a separate section or separate notebook. Add any words that you look up in the dictionary, as well as from word lists. Review your word lists regularly.

Photocopying or printing off word lists from the Internet or handouts is not the same. Actually writing out the word and a few notes on the definition is an important process for imprinting the word in your brain. Writing out the word and definition in your New Word Journal, forces you to concentrate and focus on the new word. Hitting PRINT or pushing the button on the photocopier does not do the same thing.

MEANING IN CONTEXT ANSWER SHEET

	A	B	C	D	E		A	B	C	D	E
1	○	○	○	○	○	21	○	○	○	○	○
2	○	○	○	○	○	22	○	○	○	○	○
3	○	○	○	○	○	23	○	○	○	○	○
4	○	○	○	○	○	24	○	○	○	○	○
5	○	○	○	○	○	25	○	○	○	○	○
6	○	○	○	○	○
7	○	○	○	○	○
8	○	○	○	○	○
9	○	○	○	○	○
10	○	○	○	○	○
11	○	○	○	○	○
12	○	○	○	○	○
13	○	○	○	○	○
14	○	○	○	○	○
15	○	○	○	○	○
16	○	○	○	○	○
17	○	○	○	○	○
18	○	○	○	○	○
19	○	○	○	○	○
20	○	○	○	○	○

Meaning in Context

Meaning in context is a powerful tool for learning vocabulary. You make an educated guess of the meaning from the context of the sentence. With meaning in context questions, also called sentence completion, you don't have to know the exact meaning - just an approximate meaning to answer the question.

This is also true is when reading. Sometimes it is necessary to know the exact meaning. Other times, the exact meaning is not important and you can make an educated guess from the context and continue reading.

The meaning in context exercises below give you practice making guesses about the meaning.

Directions: For each of the questions below, choose the word with the meaning best suited to the sentence based on the context.

1. When Joe broke his _____ in a skiing accident, his entire leg was in a cast.

    a. Ankle

    b. Humerus

    c. Wrist

    d. Femur

2. Alan had to learn the _____ system of numbering when his family moved to Great Britain.

    a. American

    b. Decimal

    c. Metric

    d. Fingers and toes

3. After Lisa's aunt had her tenth child, Lisa found that she had more than twenty _____ .

    a. Uncles

    b. Friends

    c. Stepsisters

    d. Cousins

4. Although he had flown many times, this was his first flight in a _____ .

    a. Helicopter

    b. Kite

    c. Train

    d. Subway car

5. George is very serious about his _____, and recently joined the American Scholastic Association.

    a. Schoolwork

    b. Cooking

    c. Travelling

    d. Athletics

6. She was a rabid Red Sox fan, attending every game, and demonstrating her _____ by cheering more loudly than anyone else.

    a. Knowledge

    b. Boredom

    c. Commitment

    d. Enthusiasm

7. When Craig's dog was struck by a car, he rushed his pet to the _____ .

    a. Emergency room

    b. Doctor

    c. Veterinarian

    d. Podiatrist

8. After she received her influenza vaccination, Nan thought that she was _____ to the common cold.

    a. Immune

    b. Susceptible

    c. Vulnerable

    d. At risk

9. Paul's rose bushes were being destroyed by Japanese beetles, so he invested in a good _____.

    a. Fungicide

    b. Fertilizer

    c. Sprinkler

    d. Pesticide

10. The last time that the crops failed, the entire nation experienced months of _____.

    a. Famine

    b. Harvest

    c. Plenitude

    d. Disease

11. Because of a pituitary dysfunction, Karl lacked the necessary _____ to grow as tall as his father.

    a. Glands

    b. Hormones

    c. Vitamins

    d. Testosterone

12. Because of its colorful fall _____ , the maple is my favorite tree.

    a. Growth

    b. Branches

    c. Greenery

    d. Foliage

13. When Mr. Davis returned from southern Asia, he told us about the _____ that sometimes swept the area, bringing torrential rain.

    a. Monsoons

    b. Hurricanes

    c. Blizzards

    d. Floods

14. Is it true that _____ always grows on the north side of trees?

    a. Lichens

    b. Moss

    c. Ferns

    d. Ground cover

15. You can _____ some fires by covering them with dirt, while others require foam or water.

    a. Extinguish
    b. Distinguish
    c. Ignite
    d. Lessen

16. Through powerful fans that circulate the heat over the food, _____ ovens work very efficiently.

    a. Microwave
    b. Broiler
    c. Convection
    d. Pressure

17. Because of the growing use of _____ as a fuel, corn production has greatly increased.

    a. Alcohol
    b. Ethanol
    c. Natural gas
    d. Oil

18. In heavily industrialized areas, the air pollution causes many _____ diseases.

    a. Respiratory
    b. Cardiac
    c. Alimentary
    d. Circulatory

19. Because hydroelectric power is a _____ source of energy, its use is considered a green energy.

    a. Significant
    b. Disposable
    c. Renewable
    d. Reusable

20. The process required the use of highly _____ liquids, so fire extinguishers were everywhere in the factory.

    a. Erratic
    b. Combustible
    c. Inflammable
    d. Neutral

21. I still don't know exactly. That isn't _____ evidence.

    a. Undeterred
    b. Unrelenting
    c. Unfortunate
    d. Conclusive

22. He could manipulate the coins in his fingers very _____.

    a. Brazenly
    b. Eloquently
    c. Boisterously
    d. Deftly

23. His investment scheme _____ many serious investors, who lost money.

   a. Helped
   b. Vindicated
   c. Duped
   d. Reproved

24. When we go to a party, we always _____ a driver.

   a. Feign
   b. Exploit
   c. Dote
   d. Designate

25. This new evidence should _____ any doubts.

   a. Dispel
   b. Dispense
   c. Evaluate
   d. Diverse

ANSWER KEY

1. D
Femur NOUN A thighbone.

2. C
Metric System a system of measurements that is based on the base units of the meter/metre, the kilogram, the second, the ampere, the kelvin, the mole, and the candela.

3. D
Cousins NOUN the son or daughter of a person's uncle or aunt; a first cousin.

4. A
Helicopter

5. B
Schoolwork

6. D
Enthusiasm NOUN intensity of feeling; excited interest or eagerness.

7. C
Veterinarian NOUN medical doctor who treats non-human animals.

8. A
Immune ADJECTIVE protected by inoculation, or due to innate resistance to pathogens.

9. D
Pesticide NOUN a substance, usually synthetic although sometimes biological, used to kill or contain the activities of pests.

10. A
Famine NOUN a period of extreme shortage of food in a region.

11. B
Hormones NOUN any substance produced by one tissue and conveyed by the bloodstream to another to effect physiological activity.

12. D
Foliage NOUN the leaves of plants.

13. A
Monsoons NOUN tropical rainy season when the rain lasts for several months with few interruptions.

14. B
Moss NOUN any of various small green plants growing on the ground or on the surfaces of trees, stones etc.

15. A
Extinguish NOUN to put out, as in fire; to end burning; to quench.

16. C
Convection NOUN the vertical movement of heat and moisture.

17. B
Ethanol NOUN a type of alcohol used as fuel.

18. A
Respiratory NOUN relating to respiration; breathing.

19. D
Reusable NOUN able to be used again; especially after salvaging or special treatment or processing.

20. B
Combustible NOUN capable of burning.

21. D
Conclusive ADJECTIVE providing an end to something; decisive.

22. D
Deftly ADVERB quickly and neatly in action.

23. C
Dupe VERB to swindle, deceive, or trick.

24. D
Designate ADJECTIVE appointed; chosen.

25. A
Dispel VERB to drive away by scattering, or so to cause to vanish; to clear away.

The Top 100 Common Vocabulary

Learning vocabulary, especially in a hurry for an exam, means that you will be making friends with a lot of different word lists. Below is a word list of top 100 "must know" vocabulary to get you started.

When studying word lists, think of different ways to mix-it-up. Work with a friend or a study group and compare word lists and test each other, or make flash cards.

1. **Abate** VERB reduce or lesson.
2. **Abandon** VERB to give up completely.
3. **Aberration** NOUN something unusual, different from the norm.
4. **Abet** VERB to encourage or support.
5. **Abstain** VERB to refrain from doing something.
6. **Abrogate** VERB to abolish or render void.
7. **Aesthetic** ADJECTIVE pertaining to beauty.
8. **Abstemious** ADJECTIVE moderate in the use of food or drink.
9. **Anachronistic** ADJECTIVE out of the context of time, out of date.
10. **Acrimonious** ADJECTIVE sharp or harsh in language or temper.
11. **Asylum** NOUN sanctuary, place of safety.
12. **Banal** ADJECTIVE lacking in freshness, originality, or vigor.
13. **Bias** NOUN a prejudice towards something or against something.
14. **Belie** VERB to give a false idea of.
15. **Brazen** ADJECTIVE bold.
16. **Belligerent** ADJECTIVE engaged in war.
17. **Camaraderie** NOUN togetherness, trust, group dynamic of trust.
18. **Cabal** NOUN a small group of persons engaged in plotting.
19. **Capacious** ADJECTIVE very large, spacious.
20. **Callous** ADJECTIVE unfeeling or insensitive.
21. **Clairvoyant** ADJECTIVE can predict the future.
22. **Cantankerous** ADJECTIVE ill-natured; quarrelsome.
23. **Compassion** NOUN sympathy.
24. **Capricious** ADJECTIVE quick to find fault about trifle.
25. **Condescending** ADJECTIVE patronizing.
26. **Chauvinist** NOUN an extreme patriot.
27. **Conformist** NOUN someone who follows the majority.
28. **Clamorous** VERB loud and noisy.
29. **Deleterious** ADJECTIVE harmful.
30. **Deference** NOUN submitting to the wishes or judgment of another.
31. **Digression** NOUN straying from main point.
32. **Delectable** ADJECTIVE very pleasing.
33. **Discredit** NOUN dishonor someone, prove something untrue.
34. **Demeanor** NOUN behavior; bearing.
35. **Divergent** ADJECTIVE moving apart, going in different directions.
36. **Edict** NOUN a public command or proclamation issued by an authority.
37. **Emulate** NOUN following someone else's example.
38. **Effete** ADJECTIVE no longer productive; hence, lacking in or, worn out.

39. **Ephemeral** ADJECTIVE fleeting, temporary.
40. **Elicit** VERB to draw out.
41. **Exemplary** ADJECTIVE outstanding.
42. **Elucidate** VERB to make clear; to explain florid: ornate.
43. **Forbearance** NOUN patience, restraint.
44. **Facade** NOUN front or face, especially of a building.
45. **Fortuitous** ADJECTIVE lucky.
46. **Fallacious** ADJECTIVE unsound; misleading; deceptive.
47. **Fraught** NOUN filled with or likely to result in (something undesirable).
48. **Flaccid** ADJECTIVE lacking firmness.
49. **Ghastly** ADJECTIVE horrible, deathlike.
50. **Grimace** NOUN a distortion of the face to express an attitude or feeling.
51. **Hedonist** NOUN person who acts in pursuit of pleasure.
52. **Harbinger** NOUN a forerunner; ail announcer.
53. **Impetuous** ADJECTIVE rash, impulsive.
54. **Immaculate** ADJECTIVE spotless; pure.
55. **Inconsequential** ADJECTIVE without consequence, trivial, does not matter.
56. **Impeccable** ADJECTIVE faultless.
57. **Intrepid** ADJECTIVE fearless.
58. **Imprecation** NOUN a curse.
59. **Jubilation** NOUN extreme happiness, joy.
60. **Latent** ADJECTIVE hidden; present but not fully developed.
61. **Longevity** NOUN long (particularly long life).
62. **Maudlin** ADJECTIVE sentimental to the point of tears.
63. **Nonchalant** ADJECTIVE casual, calm, at ease.
64. **Oblivious** ADJECTIVE forgetful; absent-minded.
65. **Orator** NOUN speaker.
66. **Obviate** VERB to prevent, dispose of, or unnecessary by appropriate actions.
67. **Parched** ADJECTIVE lacking water, dried up.
68. **Panacea** NOUN a remedy for all ills.
69. **Pragmatic** ADJECTIVE practical.
70. **Paraphrase** VERB to restate the meaning of a passage in other words.
71. **Pretentious** ADJECTIVE being self important, thinking you are better.
72. **Pecuniary** ADJECTIVE pertaining to money.
73. **Prosaic** ADJECTIVE ordinary.
74. **Pensive** ADJECTIVE sadly thoughtful.
75. **Provocative** ADJECTIVE causes a fuss, inflammatory.
76. **Peruse** VERB to read carefully.
77. **Querulous** ADJECTIVE irritable, prone to argument.
78. **Radical** NOUN one who advocates extreme basic changes.
79. **Reclusive** ADJECTIVE hermit, withdrawn.
80. **Recapitulate** VERB to restate in a brief, concise form.
81. **Renovate** VERB to make new, being redone.
82. **Refute** VERB to prove incorrect or false.
83. **Reverence** NOUN deep respect.
84. **Sallow** ADJECTIVE sick.
85. **Scrutinize** VERB to look at carefully.
86. **Sanguinary** ADJECTIVE bloody.
87. **Spurious** ADJECTIVE false, untrue.

88. **Scourge** VERB to punish severely; to afflict; to whip.
89. **Substantiate** VERB to confirm, prove.
90. **Scrutinize** VERB to examine carefully.
91. **Superficial** ADJECTIVE shallow.
92. **Sleazy** ADJECTIVE flimsy and cheap.
93. **Surreptitious** ADJECTIVE secret.
94. **Tactful** ADJECTIVE polite.
95. **Tangible** ADJECTIVE real; actual.
96. **Transient** ADJECTIVE temporary, impermanent.
97. **Vanquish** VERB to subdue or conquer.
98. **Vindicate** VERB to free from blame.
99. **Wary** ADJECTIVE careful, watchful.
100. **Zenith** NOUN the highest point.

Stem Words

Probably the best way of learning new vocabulary is our "two-for-one" strategy of learning a stem word and then you can recognize two, three or more words that use the stem word. If you are studying for an exam with a vocabulary section, this is the best strategy for you.

Below is an extensive list of stem words with their meaning and examples. Following this list are 100 questions. These are divided into 2 question styles. In Part I, you are given the stem and asked to choose the meaning, and in Part II you are given the meaning and asked to choose the stem.

A Root	Meaning	Examples
ab-, a-, abs-	away	absent, aversion
acr(i)-	sharp, pungent	acrid, acrimony
aer-, aero-	air, atmosphere	aeronautics, aerosol
agri-	field, country	agriculture,
amic-, imic-	friend	amicable, inimical
ant-, anti-	against, opposed to, preventive	antibiotic, antipodes
ante-, anti-	before, in front of, prior to	anticipate, antiquarian
anthropo- anthropomorphic	human	anthropology,
aqu-	water	aquarium, aqueduct
arche-, archi-	ruler	archangel, archetype
archaeo-, archeo-	ancient	archeology, archaic
arthr(o)-	joint	arthritis, arthropod
astr-, astro-	star, star-shaped	asterisk, astronomy
aud(i)-	hearing, listening, sound	auditorium, auditory
aut-, auto-	self; directed from within	automobile, autonomy
avi-	bird	aviary, aviation
B Root	Meaning	Examples
barograph	weight, pressure	barometer,
basi-	at the bottom	basic, basis
bell(i)- belligerent	war	bellicose,
bibl-	book	bibliography, bible
bi(o)-	life	biology, biosphere
brev(i)-	brief, short (time)	abbreviation, brevity

C root Con't		
cruc(i)-	cross	crucifix, crucify
crypt-	hidden	cryptic, cryptography
curr-, curs-	run	concurrent, recursion
cycl(o)-	circular	bicycle, cycle, cyclone
D Root	**Meaning**	**Examples**
de-	from, away from, removing	delete, demented
dens-	thick	condense, density
dent-	tooth	dental, dentures
	skin	dermis, epidermis
dorm-	sleep	dormant, dormitory
E Root	**Meaning**	**Examples**
equ-, -iqu-	even, level	equal, equivalence
ethn-	native	ethnicity, ethnic
eu-	well, good	euphoria,
euthanasia		
ex-, e-, ef-	from, out	exclude, extrude, extend
exter-, extra-	outer	exterior, extrasensory
extrem-	utmost, outermost	extremity, extremophile
F Root	**Meaning**	**Examples**
-fect-	make	defect, factory, manufacture
femin-	female	femininity, feminist
feder-	treaty, agreement, contract, league	confederation, federal

F root Con't		
fid-, fis-	faith, trust	confidence, fidelity
fin-	end	finish, final
flig-, flict-	strike	conflict, inflict
flor-	flower	floral, florid
form-	shape	conformity, deformity
fract-, frag-	break	fracture, fragment
front-	forehead	confront, frontal
fug-, fugit-	flee	centrifuge, fugitive
G Root	Meaning	Examples
ger-, gest-	bear, carry	digest, gestation
glob-	sphere	global, globule
grad-, gress-	walk, step	grade, regress
gran-	grain	granary, granule
greg-	flock	gregarious, segregation
H Root	**Meaning**	**Examples**
haem-	blood	haemophilia, haemoglobin
hemi-	half	hemicycle, hemisphere
her-, hes-	cling	adhesive, coherent
hom(o)-	same	homosexual, homogenous
hort(i)-	garden	horticulture, horticulturist
hospit-	host	hospitality, hospitable
hydr(o)-	water	hydrophobia, hydroponic
I Root	**Meaning**	**Examples**
idi(o)-	personal	idiom, idiosyncrasy
ign-	fire	igneous, ignition
infra-	below, under	infrastructure, infrared
inter-	among, between	intermission, intersection
J Root	**Meaning**	**Examples**
jac- -ject-	cast, throw	eject, interject
jung-, junct-	join	conjunction, juncture
juven-	young, youth	juvenile, rejuvenate

K Root	Meaning	Examples
kil(o)-	thousand	kilobyte, kilogram, kilometer
kine-	movement, motion	Kinetic, kinesthetic

L Root	Meaning	Examples
lab-, laps-	slide, slip	elapse, relapse
lact-	milk	lactate, lactose
lax-	not tense	laxative, relaxation
leg-	law	legal, legislative
lev-	lift, light	elevator, levitation
liber-	free	liberation, liberty
lingu-	language, tongue	bilingual, linguistic
loc-	place	local, location
long-	long	elongate, longitude
lumin-	light	illumination, luminous
lun-	moon	lunar, lunatic

How to Improve your Vocabulary

M Root	Meaning	Examples
maj-	greater	majesty, majority
mal-	bad	malicious, malignant
mania	mental illness	kleptomania, maniac
manu-	hand	manual, manuscript
mar-	sea	marine, maritime
maxim-	greatest	maximal, maximum
medi-, -midi-	middle	median, medieval
ment-	mind	demented, mentality
merc-	reward, wages	mercantile, merchant
merg-, mers-	dip, plunge	emerge, immersion
meter-, metr-	measure	metric, thermometer
micr(o)-	small	microphone, microscope
migr-	wander	emigrant, migrate
milit-	soldier	military, militia
mill-	thousand	millennium, million
mim-	repeat	mime, mimic
min-	less, smaller	minority, minuscule
mir-	wonder, amazement	admire, miracle
misce-, mixt-	mix	miscellaneous, mixture
mitt-, miss-	send	intermittent, transmission
mon(o)-	one	monolith, monotone
mort-	death	immortal, mortuary
mov-, mot-	move	motion, momentum
mult(i)-	many, much	multiple, multiplex

N Root	Meaning	Examples
narc-	numb	narcosis, narcotic
nav-	ship	naval, navigate
neur-	nerve	neurology, neurosurgeon
nud-	naked	denude, nude
nutri	nourish	nutrition, nutrient

O Root	Meaning	Examples
ob-, o-, oc-, os-	against	obstinate, ostentatious
oct-	eight	octagon, octahedron
ocul-	eye	ocular, oculus
omni-	all	omnipotence, omnivore
opt-	eye	optical, optician
opt-	choose	adopt, optional
or-	mouth	oral, orator
ordin-	order	ordinal, ordinary
orn-	decorate	adorn, ornament
ov-	egg	oval, ovule

P Root	Meaning	Examples
pac-	peace	pacifism, pacifist
paed-, ped	child	pediatric, pediatrician
pall-	be pale	pallid, pallor
pand-, pans-	spread	expand, expansion
par(a)-	beside, near	parallel, parameter
past-	feed	pasture, repast
ped-	foot, child	pedal, quadruped
pharmac-	drug, medicine	pharmacy, pharmacist
phob-	fear	hydrophobia, agoraphobia
phon(o)-	sound	microphone, phonograph
plan-	flat	planar, plane
plas-	mould	plasma, plastic
plaus-	clap	applaud, applause
pod-	foot	podiatry, tripod
pol-	pole	dipole, polar
pole-, poli-	city	metropolis, politics
port-	carry	export, transportation
post-	after, behind	posterior, postscript
pre-	before	prehistoric, previous
prim-	first	primary, primeval
priv(i)-	separate	deprivation, privilege
proxim-	nearest	approximate, proximity
pugn-	fight	pugnacious, repugnant

Q Root	Meaning	Examples
quadr-	four	quadrangle, quadrillion
quin-	fifth	quintary, quintile
quot-	how many, how great	quota, quotient

R Root	Meaning	Examples
rad-, ras-	scrape, shave	abrade, abrasion
ranc-	rancidness, grudge, bitterness	rancid, rancour
re-, red-	again, back	recede, redact
retro-	backward, behind	retrograde, retrospective
rid-, ris-	laugh	derision, ridicule
rod-, ros-	gnaw	erosion, rodent
rump-, rupt-	break	eruption, rupture

S Root	Meaning	Examples
sacr-, secr-	sacred	consecrate, sacrament
sanc-	holy	sanctify, sanctuary
sci-	know	prescient, science
scind-, sciss-	split	rescind, scissors
scrib-, script-	write	inscribe, scripture
se-, sed-	apart	secede, sedition
sect-, seg-	cut	section, segment
sed-	settle, calm	sedative, sedate
sema-	sign	semantics, semaphore

sen-	old man	senator, senility
sequ-, secut-	follow	consecutive, sequence
sign-	sign	design, designate
sist-	cause to stand	consist, persistence
soci-	group	associate, social
sol-	sun	solar
sol-	comfort	soothe, consolation
sol-	alone, only	sole, solo
solv-, solut-	loosen, set free	dissolve, solution
sorb-, sorpt-	suck	absorb, absorption
spec-, -spic-, spect-	look	conspicuous, inspection, specimen
spher-	ball	sphere, spheroid
squal-	scaly, dirty, filthy	squalid, squalor
statu-, -stitu-	stand	institution, statute
stell-, stellar	star	constellation,
still-	drip	distillation
stinct-	apart	distinction, distinguish
stru-, struct-	structure, building	construction, construe
subter-	under	subterfuge, subterranean
sum-, sumpt-	take	assumption, consume
T Root	**Meaning**	**Examples**
tac-, -tic-	be silent	reticent, tacit
tang-, -ting-, tact-, tag-	touch	contact, tactile
tele-	far, end	telegram, telephone
tempor-	time	contemporary, temporal
ten-, -tin-, tent-	hold	detention, tenacious

tend-, tens-	stretch	extend, extension
termin-	boundary, limit, end	terminal, termination
terr-	dry land	terrace, terrain
test-	witness	testament, testimony
tex-, text-	weave	texture, textile
tot-	all, whole	total, totality
trans-, tra-, tran-	across	tradition, transportation
traum-	wound	trauma, traumatic
tri-	three	triad, tripod
tri-	three	triangle, trivia
typ-	stamp, model	archetype, typography
U Root	**Meaning**	**Examples**
ultim-	farthest	ultimatum, ultimate
ut-, us-	use	usual, utility
V Root	**Meaning**	**Examples**
vac-	empty	vacancy, vacuum
vad-, vas-	go	evade, pervasive
vag-	wander	vague, vagabond
vap-	lack (of)	evaporation, vapid
ven-, vent-	come	advent, convention
vend-	sell	vendor, vending
verb-	word	verbal, verbatim
vert-, vers-	turn	convert, invert
veter-	old	inveterate, veteran
vi-	way	deviate, via
V Root con't		
vid-, vis-	see	video, vision
vil-	cheap	vile, vilify
vinc-, vict-	conquer	invincible, victory
viv-	live	revive, survive, vivid
voc-	voice	vocal, provocative
volv-, volut-	roll	convolution, revolve
vor-, vorac-	swallow	devour, voracious
Z Root	**Meaning**	**Examples**
zo-	animal, living being	zoo, zoology

Answer Sheet

	A	B	C	D	E		A	B	C	D	E
1	○	○	○	○	○	21	○	○	○	○	○
2	○	○	○	○	○	22	○	○	○	○	○
3	○	○	○	○	○	23	○	○	○	○	○
4	○	○	○	○	○	24	○	○	○	○	○
5	○	○	○	○	○	25	○	○	○	○	○
6	○	○	○	○	○						
7	○	○	○	○	○						
8	○	○	○	○	○						
9	○	○	○	○	○						
10	○	○	○	○	○						
11	○	○	○	○	○						
12	○	○	○	○	○						
13	○	○	○	○	○						
14	○	○	○	○	○						
15	○	○	○	○	○						
16	○	○	○	○	○						
17	○	○	○	○	○						
18	○	○	○	○	○						
19	○	○	○	○	○						
20	○	○	○	○	○						

Stem Words Practice Questions

1. Choose the meaning of the stem word quot-

  a. How many
  b. Development
  c. Field
  d. Government

2. Choose the meaning of the stem word stu-

  a. Health study
  b. Building
  c. Stretched out
  d. On both sides

3. Choose the meaning of the stem word baro-

  a. Weight or pressure
  b. North
  c. Brief
  d. Greatness

4. Choose the meaning of the stem word bibl-

  a. At the bottom
  b. Deep
  c. Book
  d. Wood

5. Choose the meaning of the stem word vac-

  a. Pretty
  b. Stone
  c. Empty
  d. Vault

6. Choose the meaning of the stem word cand-

  a. Long
  b. Goat like
  c. Harden
  d. Glowing

7. Choose the meaning of the stem word temin-

  a. End
  b. Tenth part
  c. Leadership
  d. Move away from

8. Choose the meaning of the stem word derm-

  a. Above
  b. Skin
  c. Insane actions
  d. Fingers

9. Choose the meaning of the stem word equ-

  a. Even or level
  b. Knowledge
  c. Inside or within
  d. House

10. Choose the meaning of the stem word haem-

   a. Mental state
   b. Blood
   c. Child health
   d. Time

11. Choose the meaning of the stem word hemi-

   a. Half
   b. Air
   c. Strange
   d. Foreign

12. Choose the meaning of the stem word infra-

   a. Doubtful
   b. Foundation
   c. Strength
   d. Below or under

13. Choose the meaning of the stem word junct-

   a. Sound
   b. Join
   c. Jungle
   d. Electricity

14. Choose the meaning of the stem word lact-

   a. Shine
   b. Milk
   c. Lecture
   d. Teaching

15. Choose the meaning of the stem word lingu-

   a. Teacher
   b. Language, tongue
   c. Knowledge
   d. Tribes

16. Choose the meaning of the stem word nav-

   a. Slime
   b. Ship
   c. Join
   d. Tell

17. Choose the meaning of the stem word pac-

   a. Feed
   b. Ancient
   c. Peace
   d. Maiden

18. Choose the meaning of the stem word retro-

   a. Backward or behind
   b. Air less
   c. Kidney
   d. Nose or snout

19. Choose the meaning of the stem word rupt-

   a. Gnaw
   b. Prow
   c. Throat
   d. Break

20. Choose the meaning of the stem word sacr-

a. Sacred

b. Flesh

c. Scratch

d. Seriousness

21. Choose the meaning of the stem word termin-

a. God

b. Machine

c. Boundary or end

d. Weave

22. Choose the meaning of the stem word ultim-

a. Fruitful

b. Farthest

c. Infection

d. Shadow

23. Choose the meaning of the stem word ten-

a. Sacred

b. Flesh

c. Scratch

d. Hold

24. Choose the meaning of the stem word vi-

a. God

b. Way

c. Boundary or end

d. Weave

25. Choose the meaning of the stem word privi-

a. Fruitful

b. Farthest

c. Infection

d. Separate

Answer Key – Part I

1. A
The stem word quot- means how many, for example quota.

2. B
The stem word stu- means building, for example construction.

3. A
The stem word baro- means relating to weight or pressure, for example barometer.

4. C
The stem word bibl- relates to books, for example bibliography and bible.

5. C
The stem word vac- means empty, for example vacancy.

6. D
The stem word cand- means glowing, for examples candle and candid.

7. A
The stem word termin- means end, for example terminal.

8. B
The stem word derm- relates to skin, for example dermis and epidermis.

9. A
The stem word equ- means even or level, for example equal.

10. B
The stem word haem- means blood, for example hemophilia.

11. A
The stem word hemi- means half, for example hemisphere.

12. D
The stem word infra- means below and under, for example infrastructure.

13. B
The stem word junct- means join, for example junction.

14. B
The stem word lact- means milk, for example lactate.

15. B
The stem word lingu- means relating to language, tongue, for example bilingual and linguistic.

16. B
The stem word nav- means ship, for example naval.

17. C
The stem word pac- means peace, for example pact and pacify.

18. A
The stem word retro- means backward or behind, for example retrospect and retrograde.

19. D
The stem word rupt- means break, for example rupture.

20. A
The stem word sacr- means sacred, for example consecrate and sacrament.

21. C
The stem word termin- means boundary or end, for examples termination and terminal.

22. B
The stem word ultim- means farthest, for example ultimate.

23. D
The stem word ten- means hold, for example detention.

24. B
The stem word vi- means way, for example via.

25. D
The stem word privi- means separate, for example privilege.

Answer Sheet

	A	B	C	D	E			A	B	C	D	E
1	○	○	○	○	○	21	○	○	○	○	○
2	○	○	○	○	○	22	○	○	○	○	○
3	○	○	○	○	○	23	○	○	○	○	○
4	○	○	○	○	○	24	○	○	○	○	○
5	○	○	○	○	○	25	○	○	○	○	○
6	○	○	○	○	○	26	○	○	○	○	○
7	○	○	○	○	○	27	○	○	○	○	○
8	○	○	○	○	○	28	○	○	○	○	○
9	○	○	○	○	○	29	○	○	○	○	○
10	○	○	○	○	○	30	○	○	○	○	○
11	○	○	○	○	○						
12	○	○	○	○	○						
13	○	○	○	○	○						
14	○	○	○	○	○						
15	○	○	○	○	○						
16	○	○	○	○	○						
17	○	○	○	○	○						
18	○	○	○	○	○						
19	○	○	○	○	○						
20	○	○	○	○	○						

Stem Words Practice Part II

1. Choose the stem word that means air or atmosphere.

    a. Bran-

    b. Gen-

    c. Aero-

    d. Agog-

2. Choose the stem word that means women, female.

    a. Fam-

    b. Ward-

    c. Gust-

    d. Femin-

3. Choose the stem word that means end.

    a. Gran-

    b. Fin-

    c. Flux-

    d. Eur-

4. Choose the stem word that means life.

    a. Bio-

    b. Calcu-

    c. Ext-

    d. Ago-

5. Choose the stem word that means outermost, utmost.

    a. Frug-

    b. Etym-

    c. Larg-

    d. Extrem-

6. Choose the stem word that means at the bottom.

    a. Trid-

    b. Eco-

    c. Basi-

    d. Ful-

7. Choose the stem word that means host.

    a. Hospit-

    b. Habi-

    c. Proc-

    d. Paci-

8. Choose the stem word that means people, race, tribe, nation.

    a. Adul-

    b. Baro-

    c. Cad-

    d. Ethn-

9. Choose the stem word that means idea; thought.

    a. Cupl(u)-

    b. Stat-

    c. Ide(o)-

    d. Anal-

10. Choose the stem word that means among, between.

    a. Chang-
    b. Sta-
    c. Inter-
    d. Less-

11. Choose the stem word that means young, youth.

    a. Juven-
    b. Yot-
    c. Drap-
    d. Rabi-

12. Choose the stem word that means not tense.

    a. Hommi-
    b. Lax-
    c. –Tic
    d. Tens-

13. Choose the stem word that means mental illness.

    a. Kilm-
    b. Cher-
    c. Mania-
    d. Logy-

14. Choose the stem word that means greater.

    a. Cede-
    b. Culp-
    c. Maj-
    d. Lar-

15. Choose the stem word that means light.

    a. Lumin-
    b. Radi-
    c. Scope-
    d. Promu-

16. Choose the stem word that means eight.

    a. Kine-
    b. Zeb-
    c. Oct-
    d. Puin-

17. Choose the stem word that means movement, motion.

    a. Kis-
    b. Kine-
    c. Trid-
    d. Agog-

18. Choose the stem word that means child.

    a. Dropi-
    b. Calp-
    c. Ped-
    d. Small-

19. Choose the stem word that means fifth.

    a. Quint-
    b. Ward-
    c. Caldi-
    d. Scor-

20. Choose the stem word that means empty.

    a. Odor-

    b. Vac-

    c. Mar-

    d. Nema-

21. Choose the stem word that means animal, living being.

    a. Ery-

    b. Brat(o)-

    c. Anis-

    d. Zo-

22. Choose the stem word that means before.

    a. Hered-

    b. Pre-

    c. Part-

    d. Jug-

23. Choose the stem word that means end.

    a. Grou-

    b. Stari-

    c. Fin-

    d. Ladi-

24. Choose the stem word that means word.

    a. Nauti-

    b. Baro-

    c. Justi-

    d. Verb-

25. Choose the stem word that means sphere.

    a. Curv-

    b. Glob-

    c. Blob-

    d. Derog-

Stem Word Answer Key Part II

1. C
The stem root word aero- means air, atmosphere, for example, aeronautics and aerosol.

2. D
The stem root word femin- means relating to women, female, for example femininity.

3. B
The stem root word fin- means end, for example finish and final.

4. A
The stem root word bi(o)- means life, for example, biology, biologist and biosphere.

5. D
The stem root word extrem- means outermost, utmost, for example extremity.

6. C
The stem root word basi- means at the bottom, for example basic and basis.

7. A
The stem root word hospit- means host, for example hospitality.

8. D
The stem root word ethn- means people, race, tribe, nation, for example ethnic and ethnicity.

9. C
The stem root word ide(o)- means idea or thought, for example ideogram and ideology.

10. C
The stem root word inter- means among or between, for example intercollegiate, intermission and intersection.

11. A
The stem root word juven- means young or youth, for example juvenile, rejuvenate.

12. B
The stem root word lax- means not tense, for example laxative and relaxation.

13. C
The stem root word mania- means relating to mental illness, for example kleptomania and maniac.

14. C
The stem root word maj- means greater, for example majesty, majority.

15. A
The stem root word lumin- means light, for example illumination and luminous.

16. C
The stem root word oct- means eight, for example octagon and octahedron.

17. B
The stem root word kine- means air movement, motion, for example telekinesis, kinetic energy and kinesthetic.

18. C
The stem root word ped- means child, for example pedagogy.

19. A
The stem root word quint- means fifth, for example quinary and quintet.

20. B
The stem root word vac- means empty, for example vacancy, vacation and vacuum.

21. D
The stem root word zo- means animal, living being, for example, protozoa, zoo and zoology.

22. B
The stem root word pre- means before, for example previous.

23. C
The stem root word fin- means relating to end, for example finish and final.

24. D
The stem root word verb- means relating to word, for example verbal, verbatim, verbosity.

25. B
The stem root word glob- means relating to sphere, for example global and globule.

Word List 3 – Most Common Prefix

A prefix is a word part at the beginning of a word which helps create the meaning. Understanding prefix is a powerful tool for increasing your vocabulary because many prefix are used by two, three or more words. The word prefix contains a prefix "pre-," which means before. If you know the meaning of the prefix, you can guess the meaning of the word, even if you are not familiar with the word.

Prefix may have more than one meaning. Here is a list of 100 commonly used prefixes along with their meaning and an example of their use.

Study the list below and then answer the questions below.

Prefix	Meaning	Example
a-, an-	without	Amoral, amateur
acro-	high up	acropolis, acrobat
ab-	away	abduction, abstain
anti-	against	antidote, antivirus, antifreeze
com-, con-	together	conference, confer
contra-, contro	against, opposite	contradiction, contraception
crypto-	hidden	cryptography
demo-	people, nation	demographics
extra-	more than	extracurricular, extramural
hyper-	over, more	hyperactive
homo-	same	homonym, homosexual
im-, ir-, il-, in-,	not, without	illegal, inconsiderate,
inter-	between	Intersect, interstate
intra	within	intramural, intranet
intro-	in, into	Introspect, introduction
multi-	many	multimillionaire, multiple
mis-	bad, wrong	miscarriage
micro-	small, million	microscope, microgram
micro-	one millionth	microgram, microeconomics
mal-, mis	bad	maladjusted, malware, mistake
mini-	small	miniskirt, miniscule
multi	many	multiple, multiplicity
non-	not, without	Nonentity, nonconformist
omni-	all, every	omniscient, omnivore
octa	eight	octagon, octopus
pre-	before	preview, precedent
penta-	five	pentagon
pro-	in favor of	pro-choice, promotion

poly-	many	polygon, polyglot
quadr-, quart-	four	quadrangle, quadruple
retro-	backward	retrospect, retro
sub-	under	submarine, subterranean
semi-	half	semi-automatic , semi-
super-	extremely	superhuman, supernatural
tele-	long distance	Telephoto, telecommunication
thermo	heat	thermos
tri-	three	triangle, tricolor
thermo	heat	thermometer
un-	not, opposite	unconstitutional
uni-	one, single	unification
ultra	beyond	ultraviolet
zoo-	relating to animals	zoology

PREFIX ANSWER SHEET

	A	B	C	D	E		A	B	C	D	E
1	○	○	○	○	○	21	○	○	○	○	○
2	○	○	○	○	○	22	○	○	○	○	○
3	○	○	○	○	○	23	○	○	○	○	○
4	○	○	○	○	○	24	○	○	○	○	○
5	○	○	○	○	○	25	○	○	○	○	○
6	○	○	○	○	○						
7	○	○	○	○	○						
8	○	○	○	○	○						
9	○	○	○	○	○						
10	○	○	○	○	○						
11	○	○	○	○	○						
12	○	○	○	○	○						
13	○	○	○	○	○						
14	○	○	○	○	○						
15	○	○	○	○	○						
16	○	○	○	○	○						
17	○	○	○	○	○						
18	○	○	○	○	○						
19	○	○	○	○	○						
20	○	○	○	○	○						

Prefix Questions

1. Choose the prefix that means single or uniform.

   a. Uni-
   b. Epic-
   c. Hydra-
   d. Si-

2. Choose the prefix that means long distance.

   a. Mini-
   b. Tele-
   c. Dis-
   d. Sci-

3. Choose the prefix that means bad.

   a. Bathy-
   b. Mal-
   c. Re-
   d. Ectos-

4. Choose the prefix that means all or every.

   a. Multi-
   b. Omni-
   c. Creo-
   d. Mal-

5. Choose the prefix that means opposite and against.

   a. Contra-
   b. Deg-
   c. Erg-
   d. Re-

6. Choose the prefix that means wrong or bad.

   a. Dis-
   b. Demo-
   c. Grad-
   d. Mis-

7. Choose the prefix that means many.

   a. Poly-
   b. Pro-
   c. Pan-
   d. Recti-

8. Choose the prefix that means before.

   a. Anti
   b. Tachy-
   c. Pre-
   d. Quin-

9. Choose the best meaning of the prefix anti.

   a. Water
   b. Enemies
   c. Against
   d. Missing the mark

10. Choose the best meaning of the prefix thermo.

   a. Long distance
   b. Heat
   c. Hard
   d. Pressure

11. Choose the best meaning of the prefix intra.

a. Square shape
b. Between
c. Round
d. Border line

12. Choose the best meaning of the prefix multi.

a. Blood
b. Severe pain
c. Narrow
d. Many

13. Choose the best meaning of the prefix mini.

a. Harsh
b. Acute
c. Small
d. Larger than normal

14. Choose the best meaning of the prefix octa.

a. Extreme
b. Eight
c. Short
d. Water animal

15. Choose the best meaning of the prefix pro.

a. Extremely cold
b. Before
c. In favor of
d. Repeat

16. Choose the best meaning of the prefix quad.

a. 3-Sided
b. Four
c. Five
d. Many sided

17. Choose the best meaning of the prefix retro.

a. Related to temperature
b. Against
c. Deny
d. Backward

18. Choose the best meaning of the prefix semi.

a. Half
b. Complete
c. Related to money
d. Related to weapons

19. Choose the best meaning of the prefix ultra.

a. Double
b. Far beyond
c. Slow
d. Related to health

20. Choose the best meaning of the prefix tri.

a. Three
b. Acrobat
c. Related to time
d. Related to air

21. Choose the best meaning of the prefix un.

    a. Alone

    b. Together

    c. Opposite

    d. Agreement

22. Choose the best meaning of the prefix zoo.

    a. Same time

    b. Relating to animals

    c. Related to the forest

    d. Large house

23. Choose the best meaning of the prefix homo.

    a. Same

    b. Red in color

    c. Related to blood

    d. Hard

24. Choose the best meaning of the prefix super.

    a. Extremely

    b. Relating to animals

    c. Related to the forest

    d. Large house

25. Choose the best meaning of the prefix intro.

    a. Same

    b. Red in color

    c. Into

    d. Hard

Answer Key

1. A
The prefix uni means single and uniform, for example unification.

2. B
The prefix tele means long distance, for example telecommunication.

3. B
The prefix mal means bad, for example maladjusted.

4. B
The prefix omni means all or every, for example omniscient.

5. A
The prefix contra means opposite or against, for example contradiction.

6. D
The prefix mis means wrong or bad, for example misstep or miscarriage.

7. A
The prefix poly means many, for example polygon.

8. C
The prefix pre means before, for example preview.

9. C
The prefix anti means against, for example, antichrist.

10. B
The prefix thermo means heat, for example thermostat.

11. B
The prefix intra means between, for example intravenous.

12. D
The prefix multi means many, for example multiple.

13. C
The prefix mini means small, for example miniscule.

14. B
The prefix octa means eight, for example octagon.

15. C
The prefix pro means in favor of, for example promotion.

16. B
The prefix quad means four, for example quadruped, or four legs.

17. D
The prefix retro means backward, for example retrospect.

18. A
The prefix semi means half, for example semi-detached.

19. B
The prefix ultra means far beyond, for example ultraviolet.

20. A
The prefix tri means three, for example trilogy.

21. C
The prefix un means opposite and not, for example unconstitutional.

22. B
The prefix zoo means animal, for example zoology.

23. A
The prefix homo means same, for example homosexual.

24. A
The prefix super means extreme, for example supernatural.

25. C
The prefix intro means into, for example introspect.

Word List 4 – Most Common Synonyms

Synonyms, like prefix and stem words are a great two-for-one strategy for improving your vocabulary fast. Below is a list of the most common synonyms followed by 30 questions.

Word	Synonym	Synonym
Amazing	Extraordinary	Astonishing
Aggravate	Infuriate	Annoy
Arrogant	Imperious	Disdainful
Answer	Respond	Reply
Antagonist	Enemy	Adversary
Attain	Achieve	Reach
Benevolence	Kindness	Charitable
Berate	Disapprove	Criticize
Beautiful	Gorgeous	Attractive
Big	Gigantic	Enormous
	Loud	Rowdy
Boring	Uninteresting	Dull
Budget	Plan	Allot
Contradict	Oppose	Deny
Category	Division	Classification
Complete	Comprehensive	Total
	Prominent	Bold
Catch	Seize	Capture
Chubby	Fat	Plump
Congenial	Pleasant	Friendly
Criticize	Berate	Belittle
Delicious	Delectable	Appetizing
Describe	Portray	Picture
Destroy	Ruin	Wreck
Dwindle	Diminish	Abate
Difference	Contrast	Dissimilarity
Decay	Rot	Decompose
Decent	Pure	Honorable
Decipher	Decode	Decrypt
Eager	Enthusiastic	Willing

Word	Synonym	Synonym
Elaborate	Enhance	Explain
Explain	Elaborate	Elucidate
Eccentric	Weird	Odd
Embezzle	Misappropriate	Steal
Fastidious	Exacting	Particular
Flatter	Praise	Compliment
Fantasy	Imagine	Day dream
	Caress	Stroke
Furious	Raging	Angry
Good	Sound	Excellent
Genuine	Real	Actual
Gay	Happy	Cheerful
Ghastly	Horrible	Gruesome
Handicap	Disadvantage	Disability
Haughty	Proud	Arrogant
Hypocrisy	Pretense	Duplicity
Humiliate	Shame	Humble
	Unconquerable	Indomitable
Interesting	Captivating	Engaging
Illicit	Illegal	Unlawful
Immaterial	Irrelevant	Unimportant
Illustrious	Famous	Noble
Impregnable	Unconquerable	Unbeatable
Incoherent	Jumbled	Confused
Dishonest	Deceitful	Duplicitous
Itinerary	Schedule	Route
Intrusive	Invasive	Nosy
Jargon	Slang	Lingo
Jovial	Jolly	Genial
Juvenile	Immature	Adolescent
Justification	Reason	Excuse
Justification	Scoff	Mock
Jostle	Shove	Push
Keep	Hold	Retain
Keen	Sharp	Acute
Keel	Swagger	Reel
Look	Gaze	Inspect
Little	Tiny	Small

Word	Synonym	Synonym
Limitation	Constraint	Boundary
Least	Lowest	Minimum
Malice	Bitterness	Spite
Match	Identical	Correspond
Memorial	Commemorate	Monument
Meager	Bare	Scanty
Memento	Gift	Keepsake
Necessary	Required	Essential
Negotiate	Scheme	Bargain
Novice	Learner	Beginner
Narrate	Disclose	Tell
Negligible	Unimportant	Insignificant
Obstinate	Adamant	Stubborn
Omen	Premonition	Foreboding
Opulence	Abundance	Wealth
Omit	Exclude	Disregard
Perplex	Confuse	Astonish
Parcel	Bundle	Package
Pause	Wait	Break
Plight	Situation	Scenario
Quack	Fake	Charlatan
Quip	Joke	Jest
Renown	Famous	Popular
Radiate	Emanate	Effuse
Run	Accelerate	Dash
Romantic	Amorous	Loving
Rebel	Dissent	Renegade
Reconcile	Harmonize	Conciliate
Render	Give	Present
Sanction	Authorize	Approve
Satisfy	Sate	Gratify
Strong	Powerful	Hard
Sealed	Stroll	Walk
Shackle	Retrain	Confine
Saunter	Shut	Close
Terminate	End	Finish
True	Accurate	Factual
Thrive	Prosper	Progress

Word	Synonym	Synonym
Tumult	Confusion	Disturbance
Tacit	Implicit	Implied
Terminate	End	Finish
Thaw	Unfreeze	Defrost
Update	Modernize	Renew
Ultimate	Supreme	Eventual
Uncanny	Mysterious	Spooky
Valid	Accurate	Legitimate
Verify	Validate	Certify
Vacate	Quit	Resign
Various	Assortment	Diverse
Wrath	Rage	Fury
Weird	Strange	Odd
Yearly	Annually	Year by year
Yank	Pull	Draw
Yearn	Long for	Desire
Zealous	Enthusiastic	Dedicated
Zoom	Speed off	Hurry

SYNONYM PRACTICE QUESTION ANSWER SHEET

	A	B	C	D	E		A	B	C	D	E
1	○	○	○	○	○	21	○	○	○	○	○
2	○	○	○	○	○	22	○	○	○	○	○
3	○	○	○	○	○	23	○	○	○	○	○
4	○	○	○	○	○	24	○	○	○	○	○
5	○	○	○	○	○	25	○	○	○	○	○
6	○	○	○	○	○	26	○	○	○	○	○
7	○	○	○	○	○	27	○	○	○	○	○
8	○	○	○	○	○	28	○	○	○	○	○
9	○	○	○	○	○	29	○	○	○	○	○
10	○	○	○	○	○	30	○	○	○	○	○
11	○	○	○	○	○						
12	○	○	○	○	○						
13	○	○	○	○	○						
14	○	○	○	○	○						
15	○	○	○	○	○						
16	○	○	○	○	○						
17	○	○	○	○	○						
18	○	○	○	○	○						
19	○	○	○	○	○						
20	○	○	○	○	○						

Synonym Practice Questions

1. Select the synonym of conspicuous.

   a. Important

   b. Prominent

   c. Beautiful

   d. Convincing

2. Select the synonym of benevolence.

   a. Happiness

   b. Courage

   c. Kindness

   d. Loyalty

3. Select the synonym of boisterous.

   a. Loud

   b. Soft

   c. Gentle

   d. Warm

4. Select the synonym of fondle.

   a. Hold

   b. Caress

   c. Throw

   d. Keep

5. Select the synonym of impregnable.

   a. Unconquerable

   b. Impossible

   c. Unlimited

   d. Imperfect

6. Select the synonym of antagonist.

   a. Supporter

   b. Fan

   c. Enemy

   d. Partner

7. Select the synonym of memento.

   a. Monument

   b. Remembrance

   c. Gift

   d. Idea

8. Select the synonym of insidious.

   a. Wise

   b. Brave

   c. Helpful

   d. Deceitful

9. Select the synonym of itinerary.

   a. Schedule

   b. Guidebook

   c. Pass

   d. Diary

10. Select the synonym of illustrious.

a. Rich
b. Noble
c. Gallant
d. Poor

11. Select the pair below that are synonyms.

a. Jargon and Slang
b. Slander and Plagiarism
c. Devotion and Devout
d. Current and Outdated

12. Select the pair below that are synonyms.

a. Render and Give
b. Recognition and Cognizant
c. Stem and Root
d. Adjust and Redo

13. Select the pair below that are synonyms.

a. Private and Public
b. Intrusive and Invasive
c. Mysterious and Unknown
d. Common and Unique

14. Select the pair below that are synonyms.

a. Renowned and Popular
b. Guard and Safe
c. Aggressive and Shy
d. Curtail and Avoid

15. Select the pair below that are synonyms.

a. Brevity and Ambiguous
b. Fury and Light-hearted
c. Incoherent and Jumbled
d. Benign And Malignant

16. Select the pair below that are synonyms.

a. Congenial and Pleasant
b. Distort and Similar
c. Valuable and Rich
d. Asset and Liability

17. Select the pair below that are synonyms.

a. Circumstance and Plan
b. Negotiate and Scheme
c. Ardent and Whimsical
d. Plight and Situation

18. Select the pair below that are synonyms.

a. Berate and Criticize
b. Unspoken and Unknown
c. Tenet and Favor
d. Turf and Seashore

19. Select the pair below that are synonyms.

a. Adequate and Inadequate
b. Sate and Satisfy
c. Sufficient and Lacking
d. Spectator and Teacher

20. Select the pair below that are synonyms.

    a. Pensive and Alibi

    b. Terminate and End

    c. Plot and Point

    d. Jaded and Honest

Choose the synonym of the underlined word

21. I cannot wait to try some of the <u>delectable</u> dishes served in the new restaurant.

    a. Unique

    b. Expensive

    c. New

    d. Delicious

22. Can you <u>describe</u> the character of Juliet in the play?

    a. Report

    b. Portray

    c. State

    d. Draw

23. The soldiers <u>destroyed</u> the rebel's camp.

    a. Ruined

    b. Ended

    c. Fixed

    d. Conquered

24. There is a big <u>difference</u> in Esther Pete's grades.

    a. Complication

    b. Dissimilarity

    c. Minus

    d. Increase

25. I can <u>attain</u> my goals in life when I study hard.

    a. Finish

    b. Forget

    c. Effect

    d. Achieve

26. The lecture was so <u>boring</u> everybody was starting to get sleepy.

    a. Uninteresting

    b. Sensible

    c. Fast

    d. Exciting

27. The <u>eager</u> crowd yelled and cheered for their favorite team during the basketball tournament.

    a. Bored

    b. Uninterested

    c. Angry

    d. Enthusiastic

28. The government is planning to end famine through mass food production.

    a. Close

    b. Avoid

    c. Stop

    d. Start

29. Children enjoy playing in the park with their playmates.

    a. Dislike

    b. Relish

    c. Spend

    d. Uninterested

30. Can you elaborate on the reason behind your tardiness?

    a. Define

    b. Correct

    c. Explain

    d. Interpret

Answer Key

1. B
Conspicuous and prominent are synonyms.

2. C
Benevolence and kindness are synonyms.

3. A
Boisterous and loud are synonyms.

4. B
Fondle and caress are synonyms.

5. A
Impregnable and unconquerable are synonyms.

6. C
Antagonist and enemy are synonyms.

7. C
Memento and gift are synonyms.

8. D
Insidious and deceitful are synonyms.

9. A
Itinerary and schedule are synonyms.

10. B
Illustrious and noble are synonyms.

11. A
Jargon and slang are synonyms.

12. A
Render and give are synonyms.

13. B
Intrusive and invasive are synonyms.

14. A
Renowned and popular are synonyms.

15. C
Incoherent and jumbled are synonyms.

16. A
Congenial and pleasant are synonyms.

17. D
Plight and situation are synonyms.

18. A
Berate and criticize are synonyms.

19. B
Sate and satisfy are synonyms.

20. B
Terminate and end are synonyms.

21. D
Delectable and delicious are synonyms.

22. B
Describe and portray are synonyms.

23. A
Destroy and ruin are synonyms.

24. B
Difference and dissimilarity are synonyms.

25. D
Attain and achieve are synonyms.

26. A
Boring and uninteresting are synonyms.

27. D
Eager and enthusiastic are synonyms.

28. C
End and stop are synonyms.

29. B
Enjoy and relish are synonyms.

30. C
Elaborate and explain are synonyms.

Word List 5 – Most Common Antonyms

Antonyms, like synonyms and stems, are a great two-for-one strategy for increasing your vocabulary. Below is a list of the most common antonyms, following by practice questions.

Word	Antonym	Antonym
Abundant	Scarce	Insufficient
Abnormal	Standard	Normal
Advance	Retreat	Recoil
Aimless	Directed	Motivated
Absurd	Sensible	Wise
Authentic	Imitation	Fake
Benevolence	Animosity	Indifference
Bloodless	Sensitive	Feeling
Blissful	Miserable	Sorrowful
Brilliant	Dulled	Dark
Certainty	Uncertainty	Doubtful
Capable	Inept	Incompetent
Cease	Begin	Commence
Charge	Discharge	Exonerate
Cohesive	Weak	Yielding
Console	Aggravate	Annoy
Confused	Enlightened	Attentive
Captivity	Liberty	Freedom
Diligent	Negligent	Languid
Dreadful	Pleasant	Pleasing
Decisive	Procrastinating	Indecisive
Deranged	Sane	Sensible
Disable	Enable	Assist
Discord	Harmony	Cooperation
Disjointed	Connected	Attached
Dogmatic	Flexible	Amenable
Erratic	Consistent	Dependable
Ecstatic	Despaired	Tormented
Eligible	Improper	Unfit
Escalate	Diminish	Decrease

Word	Antonym	Antonym
Elusive	Confronting	Attracting
Exhibit	Conceal	Hide
Fidelity	Disloyalty	Infidelity
Factual	Imprecise	Incorrect
Fearful	Courageous	Brave
Famous	Obscure	Unknown
Gaunt	Plump	Thick
Graceful	Awkward	Careless
Goodness	Meanness	Wickedness
Glamorous	Irritating	Offensive
Hard	Soft	Pliable
Hoarse	Smooth	Pleasing
Hidden	Bare	Exposed
Hearty	Apathetic	Lethargic
Harmful	Harmless	Safe
Harsh	Mild	Gentle
Idiotic	Smart	Intelligent
Idle	Busy	Working
Illegal	Lawful	Authorized
Illicit	Legal	Lawful
Illuminate	Obfuscate	Confuse
Immense	Tiny	Small
Intimate	Formal	Unfriendly
Identical	Opposite	Different
Immense	Minute	Tiny
Justice	Lawlessness	Unfairness
Jealous	Content	Trusting
Joyful	Sorrowful	Sad
Jumpy	Composed	Collected
Knack	Inability	Ineptitude
Kill	Create	Bear
Keen	Uninterested	Reluctant
Laughable	Serious	Grave
Latter	Former	First
Legible	Unreadable	Unclear
Literal	Figurative	Metaphorical
Loathe	Love	Like
Legendary	Factual	True

Vocabulary

Word	Antonym	Antonym
Large	Little	Small
Miserable	Cheerful	Joyful
Moderate	Excessive	Unrestrained
Magical	Boring	Ordinary
Minor	Major	Significant
Myriad	Few	Scant
Narrow	Broad	Wide
Nasty	Pleasant	Magnificent
Nimble	Awkward	Clumsy
Optional	Compulsory	Required
Operational	Inactive	Inoperative
Optimistic	Pessimistic	Doubtful
Ordinary	Abnormal	Uncommon
Pester	Delight	Please
Penalize	Forgive	Reward
Placate	Agitate	Upset
Practical	Unfeasible	Unrealistic
Pensive	Shallow	Ignorant
Queasy	Comfortable	Satisfied
Quietly	Loudly	Audibly
Quirky	Conventional	Normal
Qualified	Unqualified	Incapable
Rapid	Slow	Leisurely
Refuse	Agree	Assent
Reluctant	Enthusiastic	Excited
Romantic	Realistic	Pragmatic
Ridicule	Flatter	Praise
Refresh	Damage	Ruin
Rough	Level	Smooth
Sacrifice	Refuse	Hold
Sadistic	Humane	Kind
Sane	Deranged	Insane
Save	Spend	Splurge
Scarce	Abundant	Plenty
Scorn	Approve	Delight
Scatter	Gather	Collect
Shrink	Expand	Grow
Simple	Complex	Complicated

Word	Antonym	Antonym
Stingy	Generous	Bountiful
Sterile	Dirty	Infected
Tedious	Interesting	Exciting
Tactful	Indiscreet	Careless
Tough	Weak	Vulnerable
Transparent	Opaque	Cloudy
Terminate	Initiate	Start
Truth	Lie	Untruth
Understand	Misunderstand	Misinterpret
Usable	Useless	Unfit
Validate	Veto	Reject
Vanquish	Endorse	Surrender
Vanish	Appear	Materialize
Vicious	Gentle	Nice
Vice	Virtue	Propriety
Villain	Hero	Savior
Vulnerable	Strong	Powerful
Wary	Reckless	Careless
Wasteful	Frugal	Thrifty
Wane	Grow	Increase
Weary	Lively	Energetic
Young	Old	Mature
Yonder	Nearby	Close
Zealous	Lethargic	Unenthusiastic

ANTONYM PRACTICE ANSWER SHEET

Antonym Practice Questions

1. Choose the antonym pair.

   a. Abundant and Scarce

   b. Several and Plenty

   c. Analysis and Review

   d. Obtrusive and Hierarchical

2. Choose the antonym pair.

   a. Bully and Animal

   b. Teary-eyed and Gentle

   c. Tough and Weak

   d. Strong and Massive

3. Choose the antonym pair.

   a. Illuminate and Obfuscate

   b. Resonance and Significance

   c. Resonate and Justify

   d. Rationalize and Practice

4. Choose the antonym pair.

   a. Simple and Complex

   b. Plain and Plaid

   c. Shy and Sinister

   d. Vibrant and Cheery

5. Choose the antonym pair.

   a. Elevate and Escalate

   b. Exhibit and Conceal

   c. Boast and Brood

   d. Show and Contest

6. Choose the antonym pair.

   a. Strict and Tight

   b. Hurtful and Offensive

   c. Unpleasant and Mean

   d. Stingy and Generous

7. Choose the antonym pair.

   a. New and Torn

   b. Advance and Retreat

   c. Next and Last

   d. Followed and Continued

8. Choose the antonym pair.

   a. Halt and Speed

   b. Began and Amidst

   c. Stop and Delay

   d. Cease and Begin

9. Choose the antonym pair.

   a. Scary and Horrific

   b. Honor and Justice

   c. Immense and Tiny

   d. Vague and Loud

Vocabulary

10. Choose the antonym pair.

a. Dissatisfied and Unsatisfied

b. Disentangle and Acknowledge

c. Discord and Harmony

d. Fruition and Fusion

11. Choose the antonym pair.

a. Late and Later

b. Latter and Former

c. Structure and Organization

d. Latter and Rushed

12. Choose the antonym pair.

a. Belittle and Bemuse

b. Shrunk and Minimal

c. Shrink and Expand

d. Smelly and Odor

13. Choose the antonym pair.

a. Repulsive and Repentant

b. Reluctant and Enthusiastic

c. Prepare and Ready

d. Release and Give

14. Choose the antonym pair.

a. Sovereign and Autonomy

b. Disdain and Contempt

c. Disorder and Disarray

d. Refuse and Agree

15. Choose the antonym pair.

a. Gentle and Soft

b. Fragile and Breakable

c. Vulnerable and Strong

d. Vain and Tidy

16. Select the antonym of authentic.

a. Real

b. Imitation

c. Apparition

d. Dream

17. Select the antonym of villain.

a. Actor

b. Actress

c. Heroine

d. Hero

18. Select the antonym of vanish.

a. Appear

b. Lose

c. Reflection

d. Empty

19. Select the antonym of literal.

a. Manuscript

b. Writing

c. Figurative

d. Untrue

20. Select the antonym of harsh.

   a. Mild
   b. Light
   c. Bulky
   d. Bothersome

21. Select the antonym of splurge.

   a. Spend
   b. Count
   c. Use
   d. Save

22. Select the antonym of idle.

   a. Occupied
   b. Vacant
   c. Busy
   d. Interested

23. Select the antonym of console.

   a. Aggravate
   b. Empathize
   c. Sympathize
   d. Cry

24. Select the antonym of deranged.

   a. Chaos
   b. Dirty
   c. Bleak
   d. Sane

25. Select the antonym of disjointed.

   a. Connected
   b. Dismayed
   c. Recognized
   d. Bountiful

26. Select the antonym of confused.

   a. Frustrated
   b. Ashamed
   c. Enlightened
   d. Unknown

27. Select the antonym of benevolent.

   a. Nice
   b. Mature
   c. Honest
   d. Indifferent

28. Select the antonym of illicit.

   a. Unlawful
   b. Legal
   c. Anonymous
   d. Deceitful

29. Select the antonym of sterile.

   a. Dirty
   b. Alcoholic
   c. Drunk
   d. Drug

30. Select the antonym of myriad.

    a. Many

    b. Several

    c. Few

    d. Plenty

Antonyms Answer Key

1. A
Abundant and scarce are antonyms.

2. C
Tough and weak are antonyms.

3. A
Illuminate and obfuscate are antonyms.

4. A
Simple and complex are antonyms.

5. B
Exhibit and conceal are antonyms.

6. D
Stingy and generous are antonyms.

7. B
Advance and retreat are antonyms.

8. D
Cease and begin are antonyms.

9. C
Immense and tiny are antonyms.

10. C
Discord and harmony are antonyms.

11. B
Latter and former are antonyms.

12. C
Shrink and expand are antonyms.

13. B
Reluctant and enthusiastic are antonyms.

14. D
Refuse and agree are antonyms.

15. C
Vulnerable and strong are antonyms.

16. B
Authentic and imitation are antonyms.

17. D
Villain and hero are antonyms.

18. A
Vanish and appear are antonyms.

19. C
Literal and figurative are antonyms.

20. A
Harsh and mild are antonyms.

21. D
Splurge and save are antonyms.

22. C
Idle and busy are antonyms.

23. A
Console and aggravate are antonyms.

24. D
Deranged and sane are antonyms.

25. A
Disjointed and connected are antonyms.

26. C
Confused and enlightened are antonyms.

27. D
Benevolent and indifferent are antonyms.

28. B
Illicit and legal are antonyms.

29. A
Sterile and dirty are antonyms.

30. C
Myriad and few are antonyms.

How to Prepare for a Test

https://www.test-preparation.ca/video-series-on-test-preparation-multiple-choice-strategies-and-how-to-study/

Most students hide their heads and procrastinate when faced with preparing for an exam, hoping that somehow they will be spared the agony, especially if it is a big one that their futures rely on. Avoiding a test is what many students do best and unfortunately, they suffer the consequences because of their lack of preparation.

Test preparation requires strategy and dedication. It is the perfect training ground for a professional life. Besides having several reliable strategies, successful students also has a clear goal and know how to accomplish it. These tried and true concepts have worked well and will make your test preparation easier.

The Study Approach

Take responsibility for your own test preparation.

It is a common - but big - mistake to link your studying to someone else's. Study partners are great, but only if they are reliable. It is your job to be prepared for the test, even if a study partner fails you. Do not allow others to distract you from your goals.

Prioritize the time available to study

When do you learn best, early in the day or at night? Does your mind absorb and retain information most efficiently in small blocks of time, or do you require long stretches to get the most done? It is important to figure out the best blocks of time available to you when you can be the most productive. Try to consolidate activities to allow for longer periods of study time.

Find a quiet place where you will not be disturbed

Do not try to squeeze in quality study time in any old location. Find a quiet place with a minimum of distractions, such as the library, a park or even the laundry room. Good lighting is essential and you need to have comfortable seating and a desk surface large enough to hold your materials. It is probably not a great idea to study in your bedroom. You might be distracted by clothes on the floor, a book you have been planning to read, the telephone or something else. Besides, in the middle of studying, that bed will start to look very comfortable. Whatever you do, avoid using the bed as a place to study since you might fall asleep to avoiding studying!

The exception is flashcards. By far the most productive study time is sitting down and studying and studying only. However, with flashcards you can carry them with you and make use of odd moments, like standing in line or waiting for the bus. This isn't as productive, but it really helps and is definitely worth doing.

Determine what you need to study

Gather together your books, your notes, your laptop and any other materials needed to focus on your study for this exam. Ensure you have everything you need so you don't waste time. Remember paper, pencils and erasers, sticky notes, bottled water and a snack. Keep your phone with you if you need it to find essential information, but keep it turned off so others can't distract you.

Have a positive attitude

It is essential that you approach your studies for the test with an attitude that says you will pass it. And pass it with flying colors! This is one of the most important keys to successful studying. Believing that you are capable helps you to become capable.

The Strategy of Studying

Review class notes

Stay on top of class notes and assignments by reviewing them frequently and regularly and regularly. Re-writing notes can be a terrific study trick, as it helps lock in information. Pay special attention to any comments that have been made by the teacher. If a study guide has been made available as part of the class materials, use it! It will be a valuable tool to use for studying.

Estimate how much time you will need

If you are concerned about the amount of time you have available it is a good idea to set up a schedule so that you do not get bogged down on one section and end without enough time left to study other things. Remember to schedule break time, and use that time for a little exercise or other stress reducing techniques.

Test yourself to determine your weaknesses

Look online for additional assessment and evaluation tools available like practice questions for a particular subject. Visit our website https://www.test-preparation.ca for test tips and more practice questions. Once you have determined your weaknesses, you can focus on these, and just brush up on the other areas of the exam.

Mental Prep – How to Psych Yourself Up for a Test

Since tests are often a big factor in your final grade or acceptance into a program, it is understandable that taking tests can create a great deal of anxiety for many students. Even students who know they have learned the required material find their minds going blank as they stare at the test booklet. You can avoid test anxiety by preparing yourself mentally. One easy way to overcome that anxiety is to prepare mentally for the test with a few simple techniques. **Do not procrastinate**

Study the material for the test when it becomes available, and continue to review the material until the test day. By waiting until the last minute and trying to cram for the test the night before, you actually increase anxiety. This leads to negative self-talk, which becomes self-fulfilling. Telling yourself "I can't learn this. I am going to fail" is a pretty sure indication that you are right.

Positive self-talk.

Positive self-talk drowns out negative self-talk and to increases your confidence level. Whenever you begin feeling overwhelmed or anxious about the test, remind yourself that you have studied enough, you know the material and that you will pass the test. Both negative and positive self-talk are really just your fantasy, so why not choose to be a winner?

Do not compare yourself to others.

Do not compare yourself to other students. Instead, focus on your strengths and weaknesses and prepare accordingly. Regardless of how others perform, your performance is the only one that matters to your grade. Comparing yourself to others increases your anxiety and negative self-talk before the test.

Visualize.

Make a mental image of yourself taking the test. You know the answers and feel relaxed. Visualize doing well on the test and having no problems with the material. Visualizations can increase your confidence and decrease the anxiety you might otherwise feel before the test. Instead of thinking of this as a test, see it as an opportunity to demonstrate what you have learned!

Avoid negativity.

Worry is contagious and viral - once it gets started it builds on itself. Cut it off before it gets to be a problem. Even if you are relaxed and confident, being around anxious, worried classmates might cause you to start feeling anxious. Before the test, tune out the fears of classmates. Feeling anxious and worried before an exam is normal, and every student experiences those feelings at some point. But you cannot allow these feelings to interfere with your performance. Practicing mental preparation techniques and remembering that the test is not the only measure of your academic performance will ease your anxiety and ensure that you perform at your best.

How to Take a Test

EVERYONE KNOWS THAT TAKING AN EXAM IS STRESSFUL, BUT IT DOES NOT HAVE TO BE THAT BAD! There are a few simple things that you can do to increase your score on any type of test. Take a look at these tips and consider how you can incorporate them into your study time.

OK - so you are in the test room - Here is what to do!

Reading the Instructions

This is the most basic point, but one that, surprisingly, many students ignore and it costs big time! Since reading the instructions is one of the most common, and 100% preventable mistakes, we have a whole section just on reading instructions.

Pay close attention to the sample questions. Almost all standardized tests offer sample questions, paired with their correct solutions. Go through these to make sure that you understand what they mean and how they arrived at the correct answer. Do not be afraid to ask the test supervisor for help with a sample that confuses you, or instructions that you are unsure of.

Tips for Reading the Question

We could write pages and pages of tips just on reading the test questions. Here are a few that will help you the most.

- **Think first.** Before you look at the answer, read and think about the question. It is best to try to come up with the correct answer before you look at the options. This way, when the test-writer tries to trick you with a close answer, you will not fall for it.

- **Make it true or false.** If a question confuses you, then look at each answer option and think of it as a "true" "false" question. Select the one that seems most likely to be "true."

- **Mark the Question.** Don't be afraid to mark up the test booklet. Unless you are specifically told not to mark in the booklet, use it to your advantage.

- **Circle Key Words.** As you are reading the question, underline or circle key words. This helps you to focus on the most critical information needed to solve the problem. For example, if the question said, "Which of these is not a synonym for huge?" You might circle "not," "synonym" and "huge." That clears away the clutter and lets you focus on what is important.

- **Always underline these words:** all, none, always, never, most, best, true, false and except.

- **Eliminate.** Elimination is the best strategy for multiple choice answers *and* questions. If you are confused by lengthy questions, cross out anything that you think is irrelevant, obviously wrong, or information that you think is offered to distract you. Elimination is the most valuable strategy!

- **Do not try to read between the lines.** Usually, questions are written to be straightforward, with no deep, underlying meaning. Generally, the simple answer really is the correct answer. Do not over-analyze!

How to Take a Test - The Basics

Some sections of the test are designed to assess your ability to quickly grab the necessary information; this type of exam makes speed a priority. Others are more concerned with your depth of knowledge, and how accurate it is. When you start a new section of the test, look it over to determine whether the test is for speed or accuracy. If the test is for speed (a lot of questions and a short time), your strategy is clear; answer as many questions as quickly as possible.

The Nelson Denny does NOT penalize for wrong answers, so if all else fails, guess and make sure you answer every question.

Make time your friend

Budget your time from the beginning until you are finished, and stick to it! The time for each section will be included in the instructions.

Easy does it

One smart way to tackle a test is to locate the easy questions and answer those first. This is a time-tested strategy that never fails, because it saves you a lot of unnecessary anxiety. First, read the question and decide if you can answer it in less than a minute. If so, complete the question and go to the next one. If not, skip it for now and continue to the next question. By the time you have completed the first pass through this section of the exam, you will have answered a good number of questions. Not only does it boost your confidence, relieve anxiety and kick your memory up a notch, you will know exactly how many questions remain and can allot the rest of your time accordingly. Think of doing the easy questions first as a warm-up!

Do not watch your watch

At best, taking an important exam is an uncomfortable situation. If you are like most people, you might be tempted to subconsciously distract yourself from the task at hand. One of the most common ways is by becoming obsessed with your watch or the wall clock. Do not watch your watch! Take it off and place it on the top corner of your desk, far enough away that you will not be tempted to look at it every two minutes. Better still, turn the watch face away from you. That way, every time you try to sneak a peek, you will be reminded to refocus your attention to the task at hand. Give yourself permission to check your watch or the wall clock after you complete each section. Focus on answering the questions, not on how many minutes have elapsed since you last looked at it.

Divide and conquer

What should you do when you come across a question that is so complicated you may not even be certain what is being asked? As we have suggested, the first time through, skip the question. At some point, you will need to return to it and get it under control. The best way to handle questions that leave you feeling so anxious you can hardly think is by breaking them into manageable pieces. Solving smaller bits is always easier. For complicated questions, divide them into bite-sized pieces and solve these smaller sets separately. Once you understand what the reduced sections are really saying, it will be much easier to put them together and get a handle on the bigger question. This may not work with every question - see below for how to deal with questions you cannot break down.

Reason your way through the toughest questions

If you find that a question is so dense you can't figure out how to break it into smaller pieces, there are a few strategies that might help. First, read the question again and look for hints. Can you re-word the question in one or more different ways? This may give you clues. Look for words that can function as either verbs or nouns, and try to figure out what the questions is asking from the sentence structure. Remember that many nouns in English have several different meanings. While some of those meanings might be related, sometimes they are completely distinct. If reading the sentence one way does not make sense, consider a different definition or meaning for a key word.

The truth is, it is not always necessary to understand a question to arrive at a correct answer! The most successful strategy for multiple choice is Elimination. Frequently, at least one answer is clearly wrong and can be crossed off the list of possible correct answers. Next, look at the remaining answers and eliminate any that are only partially true. You may still have to flat-out guess from time to time, but using the process of elimination will help you make your way to the correct answer more often than not - even when you don't know what the question means!

Do not leave early

Use all the time allotted to you, even if you can't wait to get out of the testing room. Instead, once you have finished, spend the remaining time reviewing your answers. Go back to those questions that were most difficult for you and review your response. Another good way to use this time is to return to multiple-choice questions in which you filled in a bubble. Do a spot check, reviewing every fifth or sixth question to make sure your answer coincides with the bubble you filled in. This is a great way to catch yourself if you made a mistake, skipped a bubble and therefore put all your answers in the wrong bubbles!

Become a super sleuth and look for careless errors. Look for questions that have double negatives or other odd phrasing; they might be an attempt to throw you off. Careless errors on your part might be the result of skimming a question and missing a key word. Words such as "always," "never," "sometimes," "rarely" and the like can give a strong indication of the answer the question is really seeking. Don't throw away points by being careless!

Just as you budgeted time at the beginning of the test to allow for easy and more difficult questions, be sure to budget sufficient time to review your answers.

Here is another terrific tip. It is likely that no matter how hard you try, you will have a handful of questions you just are not sure of. Keep them in mind as you read through the rest of the test. If you can't answer a question, looking back over the test to find a different question that addresses the same topic might give you clues.

We know that taking the test has been stressful and you can hardly wait to escape. Just Leaving before you double-check as much as possible can be a quick trip to disaster. Taking a few extra minutes can make the difference between getting a bad grade and a great one. Besides, there will be lots of time to relax and celebrate after the test is turned in.

In the Test Room – What you MUST do!

If you are like the rest of the world, there is almost nothing you would rather avoid than taking a test. Unfortunately, that is not an option if you want to pass. Rather than suffer, consider a few attitude adjustments that might turn the experience from a horrible one to...well, an interesting one! Take a look at these tips. Simply changing how you perceive the experience can change the experience itself.

You have to take the test - you can't change that. What you can change, and the only thing that you can change, is your attitude -so get a grip - you can do it!

Get in the mood

After weeks of studying, the big day has finally arrived. The worst thing you can do to yourself is arrive at the test site feeling frustrated, worried, and anxious. Keep a check on your emotional state. If your emotions are shaky before a test it can determine how well you do on the test. It is extremely important that you pump yourself up, believe in yourself, and use that confidence to get in the mood!

Don't fight reality

Students often resent tests, and with good reason. After all, many people do not test well, and they know the grade they end with does not accurately reflect their true knowledge. It is easy to feel resentful because tests classify students and create categories that just don't seem fair. Face it: Students who are great at rote memorization and not that good at actually analyzing material often score higher than those who might be more creative thinkers and balk at simply memorizing cold, hard facts. It may not be fair, but there it is anyway. Conformity is an asset on tests, and creativity is often a liability. There is no point in wasting time or energy being upset about this reality. Your first step is to accept the reality and get used to it. You will get higher marks when you realize tests do count and that you must give them your best effort. Think about your future and the career that is easier to achieve if you have consistently earned high grades. Avoid negative energy and focus on anything that lifts your enthusiasm and increases your motivation.

Get there early enough to relax

If you are wound up, tense, scared, anxious, or feeling rushed, it will cost you. Get to the exam room early and relax before you go in. This way, when the exam starts, you are comfortable and ready to apply yourself. Of course, you do not want to arrive so early that you are the only one there. That will not help you relax; it will only give you too much time to sit there, worry and get wound up all over again.

If you can, visit the room where you will be taking your exam a few days ahead of time. Having a visual image of the room can be surprisingly calming, because it takes away one of the big 'unknowns.' Not only that, but once you have visited, you know how to get there and will not be worried about getting lost. Furthermore, driving to the test site once lets you know how much time you need to allow for the trip. That means three potential stressors have been eliminated all at once.

Get comfortable in your chair

Here is a clever technique that releases physical stress and helps you get comfortable, even relaxed in your body. You will tense and hold each of your muscles for just a few seconds. The trick is, you must tense them hard for the technique to work. You might want to practice this technique a few times at home; you do not want an unfamiliar technique to add to your stress just before a test, after all! Once you are at the test site, this exercise can always be done in the rest room or another quiet location.

Start with the muscles in your face then work down your body. Tense, squeeze and hold the muscles for a moment or two. Notice the feel of every muscle as you go down your body. Scowl to tense your forehead, pull in your chin to tense your neck. Squeeze your shoulders down to tense your back. Pull in your stomach all the way back to your ribs, make your lower back tight then stretch your fingers. Tense your leg muscles and calves then stretch your feet and your toes. You should be as stiff as a board throughout your entire body.

Now relax your muscles in reverse starting with your toes. Notice how all the muscles feel as you relax them one by one. Once you have released a muscle or set of muscles, allow them to remain relaxed as you proceed up your body. Focus on how you are feeling as all the tension leaves. Start breathing deeply when you get to your chest muscles. By the time you have found your chair, you will be so relaxed it will feel like bliss!

Fight distraction

A lucky few are able to focus deeply when taking an important examination, but most people are easily distracted, probably because they would rather be any place else! There are several things you can do to protect yourself from distraction.

Stay away from windows.

If you sit near a window you are adding an unnecessary distraction.

Choose a seat away from the aisle so you do not become distracted by people who leave early. People who leave the exam room early are often the ones who fail. Do not compare your time to theirs.

Of course, you love your friends; that's why they are your friends! In the test room, however, they should become complete strangers inside your mind. Forget they are there. The first step is to physically distance yourself from friends or classmates. That way, you will not be tempted to glance at them to see how they are doing, and there will be no chance of eye contact that could either distract you or even lead to an accusation of cheating. Furthermore, if they are feeling stressed because they did not spend the focused time studying that you did, their anxiety is less likely to permeate your hard-earned calm.

Of course, you will want to choose a seat where there is sufficient light. Nothing is worse than trying to take an important examination under flickering lights or dim bulbs.

Ask the instructor or exam proctor to close the door if there is a lot of noise outside. If the instructor or proctor is unable to do so, block out the noise as best you can. Do not let anything disturb you.

The PAT does not allow any personal items in the exam room. Eat protein, complex carbohydrates and a little fat to keep you feeling full and to supercharge your energy. Nothing is worse than a sudden drop in blood sugar during an exam.

Do not allow yourself to become distracted by being too cold or hot. Regardless of the weather outside, carry a sweater, scarf or jacket if the air conditioning at the test site is set too high, or the heat set too low. By the same token, dress in layers so that you are prepared for a range of temperatures.

Watch Caffeine

Drinking a gallon of coffee or gulping a few energy drinks might seem like a great idea, but it is, in fact, a very bad one. Caffeine, pep pills or other artificial sources of energy are more likely to leave you feeling rushed and ragged. Your brain might be clicking along, all right, but chances are good it is not clicking along on the right track! Furthermore, drinking coffee or energy drinks will mean frequent trips to the rest room. This will cut into the time you should be spending answering questions and is a distraction in itself, since each time you need to leave the room you lose focus. Pep pills will only make it harder for you to think straight when solving complicated problems.

At the same time, if anxiety is your problem try to find ways around using tranquilizers during test-taking time. Even medically prescribed anti-anxiety medication can make you less alert and even decrease your motivation. Being motivated is what you need to get you through an exam. If your anxiety is so bad that it threatens to interfere with your ability to take an exam, speak to your doctor and ask for documentation. Many testing sites will allow non-distracting test rooms, extended testing time and other accommodations with a doctor's note that explains the situation is made available.

Keep Breathing

It might not make a lot of sense, but when people become anxious, tense, or scared, their breathing becomes shallow and, sometimes stop breathing all together! Pay attention to your emotions, and when you are feeling worried, focus on your breathing. Take a moment to remind yourself to breathe deeply and regularly. Drawing in steady, deep breaths energizes the body. When you continue to breathe deeply you will notice you exhale all the tension.

If you feel you need to, try rehearsing breathing at home. With continued practice of this relaxation technique, you will begin to know the muscles that tense up under pressure. Call these your "signal muscles." These are the ones that will speak to you first, begging you to relax. Take the time to listen to those muscles and do as they ask. With just a little breathing practice, you will get into the habit of checking yourself regularly and when you realize you are tense, relaxation will become second nature.

Avoid Anxiety Before a Test

Manage your time effectively

This is a key to your success! You need blocks of uninterrupted time to study all the pertinent material. Creating and maintaining a schedule will help keep you on track, and will remind family members and friends that you are not available. Under no circumstances should you change your blocks of study time to accommodate someone else, or cancel a study session to do something more fun. Do not interfere with your study time for any reason!

Relax

Use whatever works best for you to relieve stress. Some folks like a good, calming stretch with yoga, others find expressing themselves through journaling to be useful. Some hit the floor for a series of crunches or planks, and still others take a slow stroll around the garden. Integrate a little relaxation time into your schedule, and treat that time, too, as sacred.

Eat healthy

Instead of reaching for the chips and chocolate, fresh fruits and vegetables are not only yummy but offer nutritional benefits that help to relieve stress. Some foods accelerate stress instead of reducing it and should be avoided. Foods that add to higher anxiety include artificial sweeteners, candy and other sugary foods, carbonated sodas, chips, chocolate, eggs, fried foods, junk foods, processed foods, red meat, and other foods containing preservatives or heavy spices. Instead, eat a bowl of berries and some yogurt!

Get plenty of ZZZZZZZs

Do not cram or try to do an all-nighter. If you created a study schedule at the beginning, and if you have stuck with that schedule, have confidence! Staying up too late trying to cram in last-minute bits of information is going to leave you exhausted the next day. Besides, whatever new information you cram in will only displace all the important ideas you've spent weeks learning. Remember: You need to be alert and fully functional the day of the exam

Have confidence in yourself!

Everyone experiences some anxiety when taking a test, but exhibiting a positive attitude banishes anxiety and fills you with the knowledge you really do know what you need to know. This is your opportunity to show how well prepared you are. Go for it!

Do not chitchat with friends

Let your friends know ahead of time that it is not anything personal, but you are going to ignore them in the test room! You need to find a seat away from doors and windows, one that has good lighting, and get comfortable. If other students are worried their anxiety could be detrimental to you; of course, you do not have to tell your friends that. If you are afraid they will be offended, tell them you are protecting them from your anxiety!

Common Test-Taking Mistakes

Taking a test is not much fun at best. When you take a test and make a stupid mistake that negatively affects your grade, it is natural to be very upset, especially when it is something that could have been easily avoided. So what are some of the common mistakes that are made on tests?

Put your name on the test!

How could you possibly forget to put your name on a test? You would be amazed at how often that happens. Very often, tests without names are thrown out immediately, resulting in a failing grade.

Marking the wrong multiple-choice answer

It is important to work at a steady pace, but that does not mean bolting through the questions. Be sure the answer you are marking is the one you mean to. If the bubble you need to fill in or the answer you need to circle is 'C', do not allow yourself to get distracted and select 'B' instead.

Answering a question twice

Some multiple-choice test questions have two very similar answers. If you are in too much of a hurry, you might select them both. Remember that only one answer is correct, so if you choose more than one, you have automatically failed that question.

Mishandling a difficult question

We recommend skipping difficult questions and returning to them later, but beware! First, be certain that you do return to the question. Circling the entire passage or placing a large question mark beside it will help you spot it when you are reviewing your test. Secondly, if you are not careful to skip the question, you can mess yourself up badly. Imagine that a question is too difficult and you decide to save it for later. You read the next question, which you know the answer to, and you fill in that answer. You continue to the end of the test then return to the difficult question only to discover you didn't actually skip it! Instead, you inserted the answer to the following question in the spot reserved for the harder one, thus throwing off the remainder of your test!

Incorrectly Transferring an answer from scratch paper

This can happen easily if you are trying to hurry! Double check any answer you have figured out on scratch paper, and make sure what you have written on the test itself is an exact match!

Thinking too much

Generally, your first thought is your best thought. If you worry yourself into insecurity, your self-doubts can trick you into choosing an incorrect answer when your first impulse was the right one!

Conclusion

CONGRATULATIONS! You have made it this far because you have applied yourself diligently to practicing for the exam and no doubt improved your potential score considerably! Passing your up-coming exam is a huge step in a journey that might be challenging at times but will be many times more rewarding and fulfilling. That is why being prepared is so important.

Study then Practice and then Succeed!

Good Luck!

Register for Free Updates and More Practice Test Questions

Register your purchase at https://www.test-preparation.ca/register/ for fast and convenient access to updates, free test tips and more practice test questions.

Online Resources

How to Prepare for a Test - The Ultimate Guide

https://www.test-preparation.ca/prepare-test/

Learning Styles - The Complete Guide

https://www.test-preparation.ca/learning-style/

Test Anxiety Secrets!

https://www.test-preparation.ca/test-anxiety/

Time Management on a Test

https://www.test-preparation.ca/time-management/

Flash Cards - The Complete Guide

https://www.test-preparation.ca/flash-cards/

Test Preparation Video Series

https://www.test-preparation.ca/test-video/

How to Memorize - The Complete Guide

https://www.test-preparation.ca/memorize/

Online Library of Student Tips and Strategies

https://www.test-preparation.ca/students-say/

www.ingramcontent.com/pod-product-compliance
Lightning Source LLC
LaVergne TN
LVHW080249260326
834688LV00042BA/1190